FOUNDATION

THE ELEMENTARY TEACHINGS OF CHRISTIANITY

J.L. Shelton

Hebrews 5:12 - Hebrews 6:2

12 For though by this time you ought to be teachers, you need *someone* to teach you **again** the **first** principles of the **oracles** of God; and you have come to need milk and not solid food. 13 For everyone who partakes *only* of milk is unskilled in the word of righteousness, for he is a babe. 14 But solid food belongs to those who are of full age, *that* is, those who by reason of use have their senses exercised to discern both good and evil.

Hebrews 6

1 Therefore, leaving the discussion of the elementary *principles* of Christ, let us go on to perfection, not laying again the foundation of *repentance from dead works* and of *faith toward God*, 2 of the *doctrine of baptisms*, of *laying on of hands*, of *resurrection of the dead*, and of *eternal judgment*.

FOUNDATION

THE ELEMENTARY TEACHINGS OF CHRISTIANITY

J.L. Shelton

Copryright © 2013 by J.L. Shelton
Published by Day 50 Publishing
Graphic Design & Layout by e2media
Edited by David Richards
Printed in the United States of America

ISBN-10: 0985228229
ISBN-13: 978-0-9852282-2-4 (pbk)
ISBN-13: 978-0-9852282-3-1 (ebook)

Unless otherwise indicated, all scriptures are taken from the KJV & NKJV™ Bible.

FOUNDATION
THE ELEMENTARY TEACHINGS OF CHRISTIANITY

ABOUT THIS BOOK

This book is the textbook version of the course "Foundation... The Elementary Teachings of Christianity". The course was developed to be accessible through multiple platforms (i.e., textbook, online e-Course, mobile app). After completing this course you should be able to:

Identify foundational beliefs of the Christian Faith

Interpret scriptures that support foundational doctrines

Examine context of doctrinal passages

Distinguish false doctrine from Biblical doctrine

Debate/Discuss basic foundational doctrines of the faith

Plan a bible study that effectively teaches foundational doctrines

Throughout this book you will find many QR Codes that when scanned from a mobile device will grant you access to additional course resources.

Scan QR Code to access e-Course

FOUNDATION
THE ELEMENTARY TEACHINGS OF CHRISTIANITY

CONTENTS

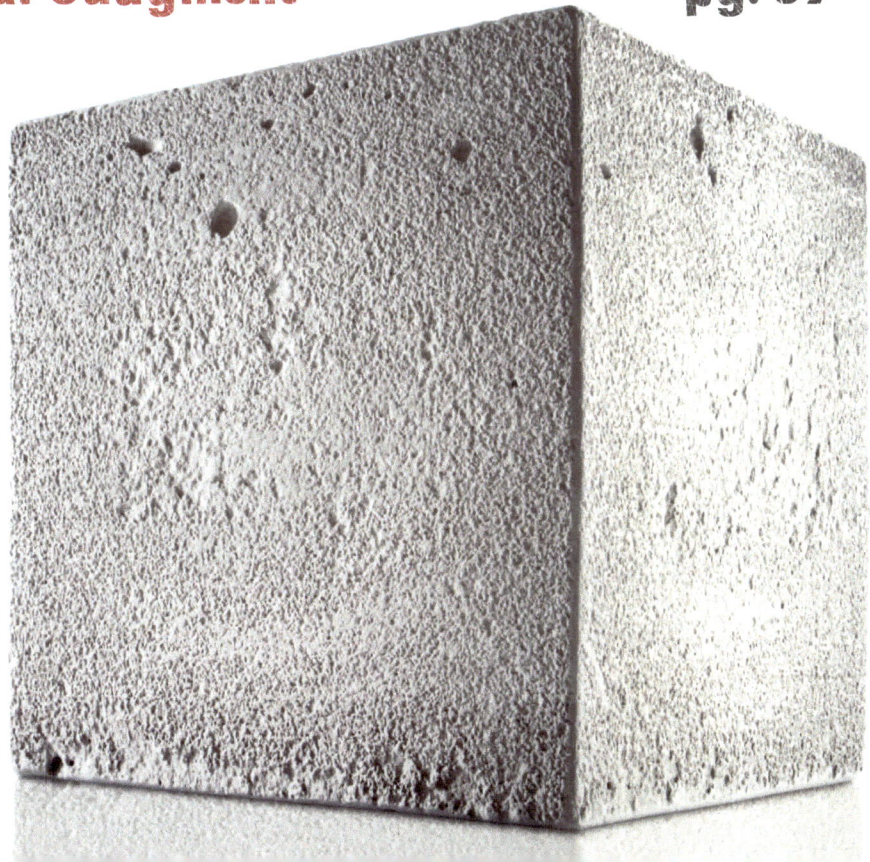

Foundation

Hebrews 6

1 Therefore, leaving the discussion of the elementary *principles* of Christ, let us go on to perfection, not laying again the foundation of *repentance from dead works* and of *faith toward God*, 2 of the *doctrine of baptisms*, of *laying on of hands*, of *resurrection of the dead,* and of *eternal judgment.*

Introduction

FOUNDATION
THE ELEMENTARY TEACHINGS OF CHRISTIANITY

Introduction

This course is intended to introduce or re-introduce the believer to the fundamental doctrines of the Christian Faith. These teachings are the very *foundation* of New Testament living and are a necessity for healthy growth and progressive discipleship. As elementary as theses teachings may seem from a distance, once engaged, the new believer and the aged believer will find a wealth of information suitable for constructing or re-pairing a doctrinal *foundation* in the faith.

In the study of any subject, the most important task is understanding the basic concept. If the basic concept of a subject is misunderstood, then every piece of information received afterwards will also be subject to this conceptual bias. For example, if one was to take an unclean glass and begin to pour purified water into it, the water that is being poured into it will cease to be purified because it has been exposed to the impurities present in its new environment. In the same manner, if the basic concept of a subject is misunderstood, then any information received afterwards will continuously be subject to this new environment.

Foundation

The first question one might ask is, what is a foundation and what does it have to do with my faith? Listed below are two general definitions for the word *foundation* which will be used to illustrate the spiritual foundation that we are speaking of.

Word Check: *Foundation*

1. **Support for building:** a part of a building, usually below the ground, that transfers and distributes the weight of the building onto the ground
2. **Support for idea:** the basis of something such as a theory or an idea[i]

The first definition describes the common structure of a building or a house and what it is built upon. This foundation is usually a flat slab of concrete laid out before any vertical construction can take place such as walls, doorways, stairwells, etc.

The second definition deals with the support system necessary for an idea or a theory to be built upon. This definition is based on the tangible perception, however it describes a mental model of the word foundation.

The Word of God in many ways illustrates the relationship between mankind and the Creator. For example the Apostle Paul tells the Church at Corinth *"you are God's building"* (1 Cor 3:9). One thing about a building is that a solid foundation is essential for the longevity of such a structure. If the foundation is not laid correctly, it will in due time have a negative *cause and effect* reaction on the building, leading to damage or possible collapse of the structure (Luke 6:46-49).

In the same manner of a physical building and its foundation, every believer existing as *"God's building"* has a spiritual foundation. This foundation is the most important element of the discipleship process of a believer. Just as a physical foundation is laid with concrete by the builders of a construction team, the spiritual foundation of a believer is laid with sound doctrine by the spiritual builders or ministers of the Gospel within the Church.

The understanding of the word doctrine is extremely important in this study and also in the walk of a believer. All throughout the epistles (Romans – Jude) the Church is commanded to teach sound doctrine. The word doctrine simply means teachings or principles that form the basis of a belief. Doctrine is considered to be a body of ideas taught to individuals for the purpose of discipleship. In scripture, doctrine is considered to be the authoritative teaching of truths to be believed. Whether one's doctrinal foundation is solid or not will play a large role in the spiritual walk of the believer.[ii]

The focal passage for this book is found in Hebrews 5:12 – Hebrews 6:2. Apostle Paul is believed by tradition to be the author of this epistle (letter).

Hebrews 5:12 - Hebrews 6:2
12 For though by this time you ought to be teachers, you need *someone* to teach you **again** the **first** principles of the **oracles** of God; and you have come to need milk and not solid food. 13 For everyone who partakes *only* of milk is unskilled in the word of righteousness, for he is a babe. 14 But solid food belongs to those who are of full age, *that* is, those who by reason of use have their senses exercised to discern both good and evil.

Hebrews 6
1 Therefore, leaving the discussion of the elementary *principles* of Christ, let us go on to perfection, not laying again the foundation of *repentance from dead works* and of *faith toward God*, 2 of the *doctrine of baptisms*, of *laying on of hands*, of *resurrection of the dead*, and of *eternal judgment*.

In this passage Apostle Paul is addressing the Church with a strong disciplinary tone. He reminds them that they have been walking in the faith for some time now and should have progressed to the level of being teachers of the faith. The context of this passage allows us to see that he is obviously not addressing non-believers or new-converts, but believers who had been in the church and had not developed properly in the discipleship process. Apostle Paul goes on to say, "*you need someone to teach you again the first principles of the oracles of God*". Notice he says "*the first principles*", which, if not properly grasped with full understanding, will hinder the growth of the believer due to an insufficient and unstable foundation. Just like the physical foundation spoken of earlier, anything built on such an insufficient or unstable spiritual foundation is bound to suffer some type of damage or collapse.

Starting in Hebrews 6, Apostle Paul outlines a clear description of what the doctrinal foundation of a believer should be. In fact he goes as far as to call them "*the elementary principles of Christ*", insinuating that one cannot go on to perfection in heavier doctrine until this foundation is laid. Listed below are the six foundational doctrines of the faith mentioned in this passage. The remainder of this book will consist of a comprehensive study of these six doctrines.

-SIX FOUNDATIONAL DOCTRINES OF THE FAITH-

1. **Repentance From Dead Works**
2. **Faith Towards God**
3. **Doctrine of Baptisms**
4. **Laying on of Hands**
5. **Resurrection of the Dead**
6. **Eternal Judgment**

Repentance From Dead Works

Hebrews 6

1 Therefore, leaving the discussion of the elementary *principles* of Christ, let us go on to perfection, not laying again the foundation of *repentance from dead works* and of *faith toward God*, 2 of the *doctrine of baptisms*, of *laying on of hands*, of *resurrection of the dead*, and of *eternal judgment*.

Unit 1

Scan QR Code to watch video

FOUNDATION
THE ELEMENTARY TEACHINGS OF CHRISTIANITY

FOUNDATION
THE ELEMENTARY TEACHINGS OF CHRISTIANITY

Hebrews 6
1 Therefore, leaving the discussion of the elementary *principles* of Christ, let us go on to perfection, not laying again the foundation of *repentance from dead works* and of *faith toward God*, 2 of the *doctrine of baptisms*, of *laying on of hands*, of *resurrection of the dead,* and of *eternal judgment.*

To understand the doctrine of *Repentance from Dead Works* first we must look at the word *repent*. The word repent comes from the Greek word *matanoeo* which is found over 30 times in the New Testament and literally means "to have a change in the way you think toward someone or something. The Old Testament concept of repentance is derived from the Hebrew word *šûb* which indicates the turning from evil to God or from idols to the one and only living God.[iii] When these two concepts are combined we see both an inner and an outer response. Thus the sinner is transformed from the inside out signifying a change that would be utterly impossible from the outside in.

A Biblical illustration of repentance can be found in Matthew 21:28,29.

Matthew 21:28,29
A certain man had two sons; and he came to the first, and said, Son, go work to day in my vineyard. 29He answered and said, I will not: but afterward he **repented**, and went.

Notice the first son had made up in his mind that he would not go to work in the vineyard that day and displayed this notion when he answered his father's request by saying, "I will not". After the colon, which represents time passing, the scripture tells us that the son *repented*. The state of repentance first took place in his mind and then it manifested into his action as the passage tells us that he went. A true change of mind will always lead to a change of action.

Say for example that I was trying to get to an out of town destination, but I was taking the wrong Interstate. No matter how fast or how far I drove, I would by no means get to my destination unless someone intervened, corrected my path, and set me on the correct route towards my destination. I would first have to come to a logical decision that I am on the wrong route, but I have not fully corrected the problem until I act on the intervention by changing the way that I am going. In the same likeness, repentance will start with a logical decision, but not until the behavior has been corrected has true repentance taken place. A change in the way one thinks will always lead to a change in action.

The Biblical mandate for repentance can fully be seen in Mark 1:14,15.

Mark 1:14,15
14 Now after John was put in prison, Jesus came to Galilee, preaching the gospel of the kingdom of God, 15 and saying, "The time is fulfilled, and the kingdom of God is at hand. **Repent**, and believe in the gospel."

This passage displays the beginning of the public ministry of Jesus. Remarkably, His first message was a message commanding the repentance of man. In essence, Jesus was telling those in Galilee to *change the way you think* and believe the gospel. This change in thought would then lead to a change in action.

Repentance is not to be confused with forgiveness. In fact, there is a clear distinction between these two words although they are often intertwined into the same reality. Biblically, *Repentance* is an action done by man towards God, while *Forgiveness* is a response by God granted unto man.

Now let's look at the concept of *Dead Works*. To help us gain a clear understanding of this concept let us first look at the word work. The most common thing that comes to mind is the duty one performs on a job. When someone is employed for a company and they are working, there is logical expectation of some type of outcome or compensation such as a paycheck. If you lift weights consistently in a weight room there is a logical expectation of muscle growth. If you spend hours cooking in a kitchen there is a logical expectation of a meal. This is simply the law of *cause and effect*.

Within that same logical expectation, *Dead Works* would be a type of work or action that leads to **Death**. Galatians 5:19-21 gives us some clear examples of what *Dead Works* are.

Gal 5:19-21
19 Now the works of the flesh are evident, which are: adultery, fornication, uncleanness, lewdness, 20 idolatry, sorcery, hatred, contentions, jealousies, outbursts of wrath, selfish ambitions, dissensions, heresies, 21 envy, murders, drunkenness, revelries, and the like; of which I tell you beforehand, just as I also told *you* in time past, that those who practice such things will not inherit the kingdom of God.

So why do these works lead to death? Because all of these works are sin, and the Bible proclaims that the wages of sin is death (Romans 6:23). Wages are considered to be the compensation one receives for performing a task. Well, according to the Bible death is the wages paid to the one who performs sin. The Apostle Paul also tells us that the sinful passions produced by the flesh and aroused by the law bear fruit to death (Romans 7:5). However, the antidote to this is the blood of Christ, which has the power to cleanse our conscience from dead works to serve the living God (Hebrews 9:14).

So what is *Repentance from dead works?*

We have just observed that repentance begins with a change of mind followed by a change of action and that a dead work is a work of the flesh which leads to death. When we put these two concepts together, we see an image of one having a change of mind about such dead works which lead to death, and making a change of action which excludes such dead works from ones lifestyle. So therefore, *Repentance from dead works* is when a believer, through the power of the Holy Spirit, makes such lifestyle changes in attempt to live a life that pleases God. However, these works are not only excluded, but they have been cleansed from our conscience so that they can be replaced with the works of serving the living God (Hebrews 9:14). *Repentance from dead works* is therefore a necessity if a believer is ever going to live a fulfilled life in God.

Without repentance there is no salvation. The Apostle Paul declares that it is repentance that leads to salvation (2 Cor 7:10). However, it must be a genuine repentance that has led to a true change in mind and action. It is impossible for one to even know the *truth* unless God first grants them repentance (2 Tim 2:25).

1.   Explain in detail what the word *Repent* means?

_____

_____

2.   What was the first message that Jesus preached?

_____

_____

3.   What is the difference between *Repentance & Forgiveness*?

_____

_____

4.   Explain in your own words, what is a *dead work*?

_____

_____

5.   Create a brief list of *dead works*.

_____

_____

6.   What are the wages of sin?

_____

_____

7.   Explain in your own words Hebrews 9:14.

_____

_____

8.   Explain in your own words Romans 7:5.

_____

_____

9.   How does one repent from *dead works*?

_____

_____

10. Which comes first Repentance or Salvation?

_____

_____

Create an outline that highlights the content covered in this unit. Be sure to include scriptures & detail. Your outline should be able to serve as a roadmap for others.

_____
_____
_____
_____
_____
_____
_____
_____
_____
_____
_____
_____
_____
_____
_____
_____
_____
_____
_____
_____
_____
_____
_____
_____
_____
_____
_____
_____
_____
_____
_____
_____
_____

Faith Toward God

Hebrews 6

1 Therefore, leaving the discussion of the elementary *principles* of Christ, let us go on to perfection, not laying again the foundation of *repentance from dead works* and of *faith toward God*, 2 of the *doctrine of baptisms*, of *laying on of hands*, of *resurrection of the dead*, and of *eternal judgment*.

Unit 2

Scan QR Code to watch video

Hebrews 6

1 Therefore, leaving the discussion of the elementary *principles* of Christ, let us go on to perfection, not laying again the foundation of *repentance from dead works* and of *faith toward God*, 2 of the *doctrine of baptisms*, of *laying on of hands*, of *resurrection of the dead*, and of *eternal judgment*.

Faith Towards God is a straightforward, fundamental doctrine necessary for a solid spiritual foundation. The word *faith* is loosely used all around the world in different cultures and diverse ethnicities. To begin, let's first look at two general definitions of the word *faith*.

Word Check: *Faith*

1. **belief or trust:** Belief in, devotion to, or trust in somebody or something, especially without logical proof.
2. **religion or religious group:** A system of religious belief, or the group of people who adhere to it.[iv]

The first definition describes the belief or trust that one displays in someone or something without any logical proof or excessive examination. For example, before you sit down on a chair you do not examine it or take a survey of people who have previously sat in the chair, instead you sit down believing that the chair will hold you. This is displaying faith in the sturdiness of the chair.

Have you ever taken a trip on a bus or an airplane? When is the last time you asked the driver or the pilot for a copy of his/her resume or driving/flying history? The answer would probably be never. Instead, you placed your trust in the person behind the wheel and believed that they would get you safely to your destination. This is displaying faith in someone.

The second definition describes a system of religious beliefs such as Christianity, Judaism, Catholicism, etc. The word *faith* can also be used to describe the group of people who profess to a particular religion. For example, people who attend Church are considered to be of the Christian *faith*.

Biblically, the word *faith* is described as *the substance of things hoped for, the evidence of things not seen* (Hebrews 11:1). Interestingly, the Bible describes *faith as a **substance***. A substance is defined as a kind of tangible matter that can be touched and felt.[v] The Greek definition defines substance as that which has foundation and has actual existence.[vi] Now of course faith is not a physical or carnal substance, but rather a spiritual substance, yet still tangible.

Faith is the driving force that gives a person the ability to believe the revelation of God and who He is. The Bible tells us that *God has dealt to each one a **measure** of faith* (Romans 12:3). In other words, God has already given each and every one of us a measure of this spiritual substance called *faith*. As believers we must protect this faith and use it as a catalyst for spiritual growth in God. The *faith* that God has given us is a responsibility and we are held accountable for what we do with it.

Let's use for example, a group of students who have been given a debit card to be used for the purpose of purchasing school supplies and books. The students have been entrusted with this card and they now have a responsibility to use it only for what it was given for. They do not have the right to use it to purchase anything else outside of the domain of school supplies and books. The catch is that even though they do not have the right, they do have the ability by free will, which was given to them in trust to spend it on whatever they choose. However, in the unfortunate event of inappropriate spending, such actions would be followed by swift and appropriate consequences by the authorities.

The Bible makes the clear declaration that *"without faith it is impossible to please God"* and that *"he who comes to God must believe that He is"* (Heb 11:6). Every man is going to place his faith in something or someone. But this substance called Faith must be placed in God. The Bible tells us that in the Old Testament King Asa became diseased in his feet and yet in his disease he did not seek God but sought the physicians (2 Chr 16:11-13). The application is that in the midst of the Kings' tribulation he chose to place his faith in the physician instead of seeking God. The end result was his death.

We see a similar story in the Gospels with a woman who had a flow of blood for twelve years (Mt 9:20). This lady had suffered many things from many physicians and spent everything she had but got worse (Mk 5:26). As Jesus was walking through the multitudes this lady reached out to touch Him because she believed in her mind that if she could touch the hem of His garment that she would be made whole (Mk 5:28). The end result was that she was healed from her ailment and Jesus told her "your faith has made you well" (Mt 9:22). Unlike the king who decided to place his faith in the physician, this woman decided to place her faith in Jesus and was made well.

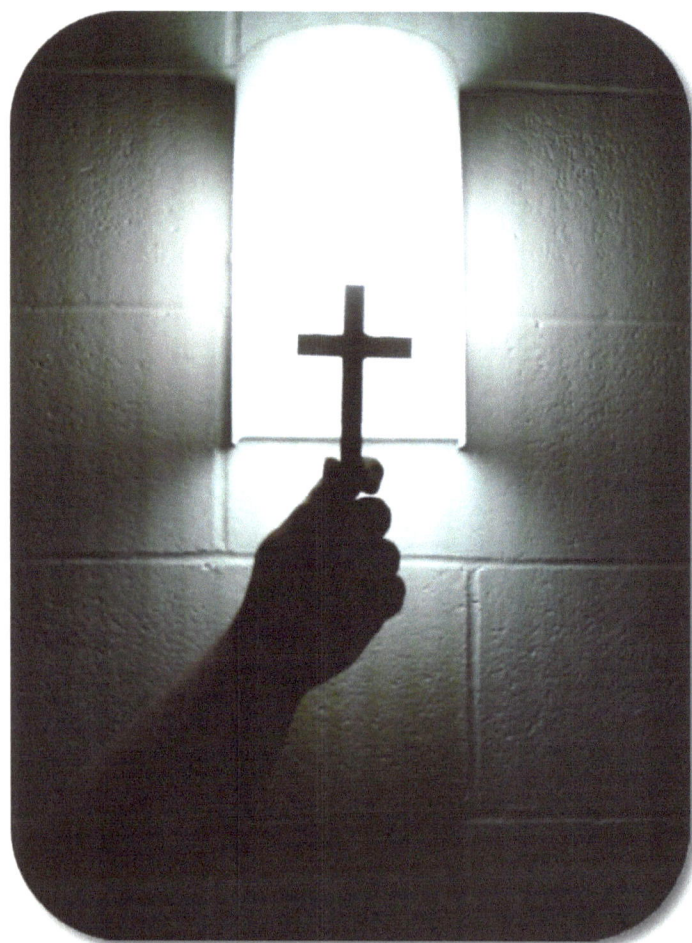

So what is *Faith Towards* God?

Faith Towards God is simply taking the *measure of faith* that one has been given and applying it towards the one and only true living God. It's obvious to see that every person has been given a *measure of faith*, whether Christian or not. This can be seen in the many religions around the world, and even within those who choose to put their faith in science. Although we are freewill creatures, mankind is still required to apply his *Faith Towards God* and not another religion, deity, or false belief system. So in essence, this substance called *Faith* was given to mankind to apply *Towards God*. The truth of the matter is that every man will place his faith in something or someone. Interestingly enough, Luke records the Apostle Paul in the Book of Acts describing the central evangelistic theme of the message that he proclaimed to the Jews and the Gentiles which included *Faith Towards God* (Acts 20:21).

Without *Faith Towards God*, an individual could never grow in the discipline of the faith or experience the blessings of God in their life. Faith is an essential substance in the life of a believer and it must be towards God. There is no shortcut or alternative route in this area. The Bible tells us that our faith should not be in the wisdom of men but in the power of God (1 Cor 2:5). It is so easy for man to place his faith in the wisdom of men because we by nature seek the visible and tangible. But God requires that our faith be in and towards Him and only Him. We must therefore nurture our faith and allow God to increase it (2 Cor 10:15) through the hearing of the Word of God (Rom 10:17)(1 Tim 4:6).

1.   What are two basic definitions of the word Faith?

     _____
     _____

2.   What is the Biblical definition of the word Faith?

     _____
     _____

3.   In your words, describe an example of Faith.

     _____
     _____

4.   What was King Asa's mistake (2 Chr 16:11-13)?

     _____
     _____

5.   Why was the woman with the flow of blood healed (Mt 9:20-22)?

     _____
     _____

6.   Why is it impossible to please God without Faith?

     _____
     _____

7.   Explain the importance of Faith in the life of a believer.

     _____
     _____

8.   In your own words, describe what *Faith Towards God* is.

     _____
     _____

9.   Give an example of how Faith can be placed in something or someone else besides God.

     _____
     _____

10. How can your faith be nurtured?

     _____
     _____

Create an outline that highlights the content covered in this unit. Be sure to include scriptures & detail. Your outline should be able to serve as a roadmap for others.

_____
_____
_____
_____
_____
_____
_____
_____
_____
_____
_____
_____
_____
_____
_____
_____
_____
_____
_____
_____
_____
_____
_____
_____
_____
_____
_____
_____
_____
_____
_____
_____

Doctrine of Baptisms

Hebrews 6

1 Therefore, leaving the discussion of the elementary *principles* of Christ, let us go on to perfection, not laying again the foundation of *repentance from dead works* and of *faith toward God*, 2 of the *doctrine of baptisms*, of *laying on of hands*, of *resurrection of the dead*, and of *eternal judgment*.

Unit 3

FOUNDATION
THE ELEMENTARY TEACHINGS OF CHRISTIANITY

FOUNDATION
THE ELEMENTARY TEACHINGS OF CHRISTIANITY

Hebrews 6

1 Therefore, leaving the discussion of the elementary *principles* of Christ, let us go on to perfection, not laying again the foundation of *repentance from dead works* and of *faith toward God*, 2 of the *doctrine of baptisms*, of *laying on of hands*, of *resurrection of the dead*, and of *eternal judgment*.

The Doctrine of Baptisms is a very intensive study and can sometimes be one of the harder concepts of Christianity to grasp whether a person is a new believer or a seasoned believer. One of the things in the above passage that is frequently overlooked by the reader is a simple plural statement that when noticed broadens the scope of this doctrine. Notice that within this passage when speaking about baptism that it reads the *doctrine of baptisms* and not the doctrine of baptism. So off top the reader should understand that this scripture is pointing to more then one type of baptism which may come as a traditional shock to many believers defying the teaching that they have embraced over the years. However, in order to fully illustrate this doctrine we must first do some background research from both the Old & New Testament.

Generally speaking, the Old Testament focuses a lot on the natural and outward expression of reality while the New Testament places a large emphasis on the spiritual and inward expression of reality. Jesus gives us a clear example of this when He taught that "whoever looks at a woman to lust for her has already committed adultery". This statement changed our perspective on the act of adultery as not only being the natural or outward act, but also the inward expression of lust (Matthew 5:27-28). If you noticed, Jesus pulled from the Old Testament to illustrate the outward expression and then revealed a deeper revelation which included the inward expression. In the same manner, we will first look back at the Old Testament and then look towards the New Testament for a deeper revelation. However it is not until we put both the Old & New Testament together that we can truly see the full revelation.

Word Check: *Baptism*

The word *baptism* has a few definitions which all play a role in helping to fully illustrate this concept into a perceivable image. One of the more general definitions of baptism is the washing or purifying by means of water. The most common definition that is usually the first to come to mind is the sacred rite involving water, symbolizing purification from sin. One of the not so common definitions, which we will frequently reflect back on, is the act of identifying one object with another.

Circumcision Of The Heart: *A type of Baptism*

In the Old Testament we find some of the central themes of the Bible in their infancy. One of the most significant themes we see is the method in which God marked His chosen people, which was by the act of circumcision. The Bible tells us that God declared to Abram(ham) that every male child among them shall be circumcised in the flesh of their foreskins, and it shall be a sign of the covenant between God and man. (Gen 17:10-13). The circumcision in the flesh was purposed for identifying Gods chosen people with Him. In other words this was the act of identifying one object with another. Just as the circumcision was the sign of the covenant between God and man in the Old Testament, God has chosen the baptism to be the sign of the covenant between God and man in the New Testament. The Baptism identifies man with the Life, Death, and Burial of Jesus Christ.

One important thing to point out is that the circumcision was considered to be the cutting away of the part of the flesh which was not necessary. Interestingly enough, the foreskin is a male genital covering which is hard to keep clean and can sometime be prone to infection. All of this plays into the understanding of what God is trying to illustrate through His Word. The Bible declares that "the spiritual is not first, but the natural, and afterward the spiritual" (Cor 15:46). God uses the natural in the Old Testament as a foundation to understanding the spiritual. While the Old Testament pointed towards the natural flesh, the New Testament points towards the spiritual heart.

Characteristics of the Relationship Between Man & God		
	OLD TESTAMENT	NEW TESTAMENT
Focal Point	Natural/External	Spiritual/Internal
Sign of the Covenant	Circumcision of the Flesh	Baptism, which is the circumcision of the heart

Colossians 2:11-13
11 In Him you were also circumcised with the circumcision made without hands, by putting off the body of the sins of the flesh, by the circumcision of Christ,

In the New Testament the Apostle Paul builds on the concept of the circumcision to reveal a deeper revelation. Contrary to popular thought, Apostle Paul wrote that he is not a Jew who *is one* outwardly, nor *is* circumcision that which *is* outward in the flesh; but *he is* a Jew who *is one* inwardly; and circumcision *is that* of the heart, in the Spirit (Romans 2:28-29). Just as Jesus pointed inward so does Paul, declaring that the inward or spiritual expression of reality has more weight than the outward expression. The question then arises, just when does this circumcision of the heart take place?

Let's take a moment to look at an interesting prophecy found in the Old Testament.

Ezekiel 36:25-27
25 Then I will sprinkle clean water on you, and you shall be clean; I will cleanse you from all your filthiness and from all your idols. 26 I will give you a new heart and put a new spirit within you; I will take the heart of stone out of your flesh and give you a heart of flesh. 27 I will put My Spirit within you and cause you to walk in My statutes, and you will keep My judgments and do *them*.

This passage is full of substance. Prophetically this passage speaks towards baptism and the giving of the Holy Spirit to dwell within man. But so often overlooked is the fact that this passage also points towards man receiving a new heart of flesh and God removing the heart of stone. This takes place at the point of salvation when one has repented and believed in their heart that God has raised Jesus from the dead (Rom 10:9). This removing of the old heart or that which was prone to infection is a type of baptism or circumcision that identifies the new believer with God.

Baptism into the Cloud & Sea: *A Type of Baptism*

One of the most popular stories in the Bible is the Exodus story of Moses and the Children of Israel. In this story the Children of Israel were divinely liberated from the bondage of Egypt under Pharaoh. God delivered them from the hands of Egypt and Pharaoh with many signs and wonders with the climax of their deliverance being the historic crossing of the Red Sea when God divided the water and the Children of Israel crossed over on dry land (Ex 14).

In the New Testament Apostle Paul reflects back on this Exodus story. He points out how they (the Children of Israel) all were baptized into Moses in the cloud and in the sea (1 Cor 10:2). The sea obviously represents and points towards the washing or purifying by means of water. The cloud however represents the Holy Spirit as we are told that the Lord went before them by day in a pillar of cloud to lead the way (Ex 13:21). This experience is what Paul is referring to when he proclaims that the Children of Israel were all baptized into Moses in the cloud and in the sea. This Old Testament type of Baptism points towards the New Testament also as Paul states that these things became our examples (1 Cor 10:6).

Baptism of John: *A Baptism of Repentance*

Malachi 3:1
"Behold, I send My messenger, And he will prepare the way before Me. And the Lord, whom you seek, Will suddenly come to His temple, Even the Messenger of the covenant, In whom you delight. Behold, He is coming," Says the LORD of hosts.

The book of Malachi is the last book of the Old Testament after which came the intertestamental period in which God did not speak for approximately 400 years until the time of Christ. In this book we find a prophecy concerning a messenger who would come before the Messiah to prepare the way. The book of Malachi goes on to say that this messenger would literally be Elijah (Mal 4:5) who was one of the great prophets of the Old Testament in which God mightily used. This messenger spoken of in the prophecy would later be revealed in the *Gospels* to be none other than John the Baptist. Jesus revealed this to both the multitudes (Mt 11:7-14) concerning John and His disciples (Mt17:12-13). In the New Testament John the Baptist is a central character in all four of the Gospels. The Bible says that:

Matthew 3:1,2
In those days John the Baptist came preaching in the wilderness of Judea, and saying, "Repent, for the kingdom of heaven is at hand!" 3 For this is he who was spoken of by the prophet Isaiah, saying: " *The voice of one crying in the wilderness: ' Prepare the way of the LORD; Make His paths straight.'"*

John came preaching a message of repentance. The Bible says that he was clothed in camel's hair with a leather belt and that his food was locust and wild honey (Mt 3:4). Jerusalem, all of Judea, and all the regions around the Jordan went out to him and were baptized by him in the Jordan confessing their sins (Mt 3:5). This Baptism is known as the baptism of repentance (Acts 13:24) or the baptism of John (Luke 7:29). The water was symbolic for the washing or cleansing of sins. This is the most popular and widely practiced Baptism traditionally throughout Church history since the time of Christ. This is the Baptism that Jesus referred to when He commanded His Disciples to *"Go therefore and make disciples of all the nations, baptizing them in the name of the Father and of the Son and of the Holy Spirit"* (Mt 28:19). Jesus Himself was baptized by John the Baptist in the Jordan River (Mt 3:16-17). But yet and still, John pointed towards another baptism.

Baptism of the Holy Spirit: *A Baptism of Power*

Mt 3:11
11 I indeed baptize you with water unto repentance, but He who is coming after me is mightier than I, whose sandals I am not worthy to carry. He will baptize you with the Holy Spirit and fire.

When we literally read the scriptures, it becomes relatively clear that there is more than one type of baptism. As John the Baptist is standing in the waters of the Jordan River baptizing the masses of people, (Mt 3:4) he lifts his voice and proclaims with boldness to the Pharisees and Sadducees who were approaching him, of He (Jesus) who would come after himself, who would baptize not with water, but with the Holy Spirit and fire (Mt 3:11). It is here that John the Baptist points towards another baptism which is known as the Baptism of the Holy Spirit.

As the time for Jesus to die drew nearer He began to comfort His Disciples with the news of the Helper in which His Father would send. This Helper is identified as the Holy Spirit who would lead them into all truths.

John 14:16
And I will pray the Father, and He will give you another **Helper**, that He may abide with you forever—

John 14:26
But the **Helper**, the Holy Spirit, whom the Father will send in My name, He will teach you all things, and bring to your remembrance all things that I said to you.

John 15:26
"But when the **Helper** comes, whom I shall send to you from the Father, the Spirit of truth who proceeds from the Father, He will testify of Me.

John 16:7
Nevertheless I tell you the truth. It is to your advantage that I go away; for if I do not go away, the **Helper** will not come to you; but if I depart, I will send Him to you.

In the book of acts we witness Jesus after His resurrection walking with His disciples, to whom He presented Himself alive for 40 days after His suffering by many infallible proofs (Acts 1:3). During this time, Jesus gives the most clearest depiction of this baptism and how it differed from John's Baptism.

Acts 1:5-8
for John truly **baptized with water, but** you shall be **baptized with** the **Holy Spirit** not many days from now." 6 Therefore, when they had come together, they asked Him, saying, "Lord, will You at this time restore the kingdom to Israel?" 7 And He said to them, "It is not for you to know times or seasons which the Father has put in His own authority. 8 But you shall **receive power when** the **Holy Spirit** has come **upon you**; and you shall be witnesses to Me…

Jesus clearly points to another baptism in this passage outside of the baptism of John. This is the same baptism that John pointed to when he said that the He (Jesus) who would come after him would baptize with the Holy Spirit and fire (Mt 3:11). The interesting characteristic about this baptism is that it comes with power.

Word Check: *Power*

The word power that Jesus used in referring to what the disciples would receive when the Holy Spirit had come upon them (Acts1:8) is derived from the Greek word *dunamis* (doo'-nam-is). This Greek word is the same word from which the word dynamite is derived. The Greek definition of this word means ability and literally the power for performing miracles.[vii] The same word that power is derived from (*dunamis*) is also translated in the New Testament into the words: might, mighty, mighty work, miracle, strength, and virtue.[viii]

The Baptism of the Holy Spirit is a baptism that equips the believer with power. This in no way is the same as the Baptism of John which is the Baptism of Repentance. John and Jesus clearly pointed to this baptism in their ministry. In the book of Acts we see the fulfillment of the Baptism of the Holy Spirit.

Acts 2:1-4
When the Day of Pentecost had fully come, they were all with one accord in one place. 2 And suddenly there came a sound from heaven, as of a rushing mighty wind, and it filled the whole house where they were sitting. 3 Then there appeared to them divided tongues, as of fire, and *one* sat upon each of them. 4 And they were all filled with the Holy Spirit and began to speak with other tongues, as the Spirit gave them utterance.

On the day of Pentecost, which was 50 days after the Death of Christ and the Passover, the Bible tells us that the disciples were gathered together with one accord in one place. And suddenly they heard a sound from heaven that they described as of a rushing wind. This sound was the coming of the Holy

Spirit which the scripture tells us filled the whole house where they were sitting. The Bible then tells us that there appeared to them divided tongues, as of fire and that one of them sat upon each of them. At this point the Bible says that they were all filled with the Holy Spirit. This is a direct fulfillment of the prophecy found in the book of Ezekiel where God said that He would put His Spirit within them and cause them to walk in His statutes (Ez 36:27). This is also a fulfillment of an Old Testament prophecy found in the book of Joel regarding the Holy Spirit.

Joel 2:28
" And it shall come to pass afterward That I will pour out My Spirit on all flesh; Your sons and your daughters shall prophesy, Your old men shall dream dreams, Your young men shall see visions.

This prophecy found in the book of Joel is what Peter used in the book of Acts to confirm what had just happened as he proclaimed to the multitude of men dwelling in Jerusalem that this is what was spoken by the prophet Joel (Acts 2:16-18). This was a momentous day because the promise and prophecies of the Holy Spirit coming to dwell within man had finally been fulfilled. Every believer could now experience the power of the Holy Spirit. The Holy Spirit empowers us and equips us for the works of the ministry and guides us into all truth.

1 Corinthians 12:8-10
8 for to one is given the word of wisdom through the Spirit, to another the word of knowledge through the same Spirit, 9 to another faith by the same Spirit, to another gifts of healings by the same Spirit, 10 to another the working of miracles, to another prophecy, to another discerning of spirits, to another *different* kinds of tongues, to another the interpretation of tongues.

Romans 12:6-8
6 Having then gifts differing according to the grace that is given to us, *let us use them*: if prophecy, *let us prophesy* in proportion to our faith; 7 or ministry, *let us use it* in *our* ministering; he who teaches, in teaching; 8 he who exhorts, in exhortation; he who gives, with liberality; he who leads, with diligence; he who shows mercy, with cheerfulness.

John 16:13
13 However, when He, the Spirit of truth, has come, He will guide you into all truth; for He will not speak on His own *authority*, but whatever He hears He will speak; and He will tell you things to come.

The significance of the New Testament believer being filled with the Holy Spirit is major. This is an experience that only very few individuals ever got the opportunity to experience in the Old Testament. The following passage is one of the rare recorded occasions where Old Testament believers were filled with the Holy Spirit.

Exodus 35:30-35
30 And Moses said to the children of Israel, "See, the LORD has called by name Bezalel the son of Uri, the son of Hur, of the tribe of Judah; 31 and He has filled him with the Spirit of God, in wisdom and understanding, in knowledge and all manner of workmanship, 32 to design artistic works, to work in gold and silver and bronze, 33 in cutting jewels for setting, in carving wood, and to work in all manner of artistic workmanship. 34 "And He has put in his heart the ability to teach, *in* him and Aholiab the son of Ahisamach, of the tribe of Dan. 35 He has filled them with skill to do all manner of work of the engraver and the designer and the tapestry maker, in blue, purple, and scarlet *thread*, and fine linen, and of the weaver—those who do every work and those who design artistic works.

In this Old Testament passage God filled a select few individuals with the Holy Spirit. When looked at closely the purpose of such an act of God can be seen. The passage tells us that they were given the gift of the Helper as Jesus called it (Him) to design artistic works, to work gold, silver, and bronze, to cut jewels for setting, to carve wood, and to work in all manner of artistic workmanship. All of this was for the purpose of the constructing and building of the Tabernacle, which was to be a worship center in which God would come down and commune with His people. In the New Testament the Apostle Paul tells us that our body is the temple of the Holy Spirit who is in us (1 Cor 6:19). In the same manner that these select individuals were given the gift of the Holy Spirit to construct a temple for the Spirit of the Lord to dwell in, we as New Testament believers have been given the Holy Spirit to construct, build, and edify the Body of believers in whom the Spirit of the Lord now dwells within.

When Does The Baptism Of The Holy Spirit Take Place?

There are many different beliefs and teachings of the *Baptism of the Holy Spirit*. Some denominations teach that a new believer receives the Holy Spirit at the point of salvation, some teach that you receive it during water baptism, while some teach that if you do not have the Holy Spirit then you are not saved. Most teachings stem from erroneous traditions and are based on dogmatic view points and not truth. However, when one looks towards the scriptures to answer these questions the answer is somewhat interesting. The *Book of Acts* gives the clearest application of the *Baptism of the Holy Spirit*. The following table is a chart highlighting documented occasions throughout the *Book of Acts* where the *Baptism of the Holy Spirit* took place. Read each passage listed in the table thoroughly and observe the chart.

When Does The Baptism Of The Holy Spirit Take Place?				
SCRIPTURE	BEFORE WATER BAPTISM	DURING WATER BAPTISM	AFTER WATER BAPTISM	How did they receive The Holy Spirit?
Acts 2:1-4			+	When the Day of Pentecost had fully come
Acts 8:12-17			+	Then they laid hands on them, and they received the Holy Spirit.
Acts 9:17-18		+		Baptized by Ananias
Acts 10:44-48	+			While Peter was still speaking these words, the Holy Spirit fell upon all those who heard the word.
Acts 19:1-6			+	When Paul had laid hands on them, the Holy Spirit came upon them

Through accurate and literal interpretation of the scripture it is observed that there is no formula or lawful time when a believer can or cannot receive the Holy Spirit. Just as Jesus said, "the wind blows where it wishes" (John 3:8). If you notice in the above table there are those who received the Holy Spirit before water baptism, during water baptism and after water baptism. Nonetheless, there are even those who had already received salvation but had not yet received the Holy Spirit, showing that one could have salvation without the Holy Spirit. One must keep in mind that just as John the Baptist stated, it is Jesus that would baptize with Holy Spirit and fire (Mt 3:11). Ultimately it is Jesus who decides when this will take place and whether or not He will use the hands of one of His servants to accomplish it or not. But Jesus, however, pointed to yet another Baptism.

Baptism into Death: *A type of Baptism*

Mark 10:38-39
Then James and John, the sons of Zebedee, came to Him, saying, "Teacher, we want You to do for us whatever we ask." 36 And He said to them, "What do you want Me to do for you?" 37 They said to Him, "Grant us that we may sit, one on Your right hand and the other on Your left, in Your glory." 38 But Jesus said to them, "You do not know what you ask. Are you able to drink the cup that I drink, and **be baptized with the baptism that I am baptized with**?" 39 They said to Him, "We are able." So Jesus said to them, "You will indeed drink the cup that I drink, and with the baptism I am baptized with you will be baptized;

The Baptism into Death is a type of baptism that Jesus foreshadowed towards in His earthly ministry. In the previous passage, the Disciples are asking of Jesus to grant unto them that they may sit on His left and right hand side in His Glory. Jesus responds by telling them that they do not know what they are asking and then questions them as to their ability to drink the cup that He is to drink and be baptized with the baptism that He is going to be baptized with. Jesus is referring to the suffering of the Cross that He would take on for the Salvation of mankind. Jesus is literally talking about the death that He would suffer.

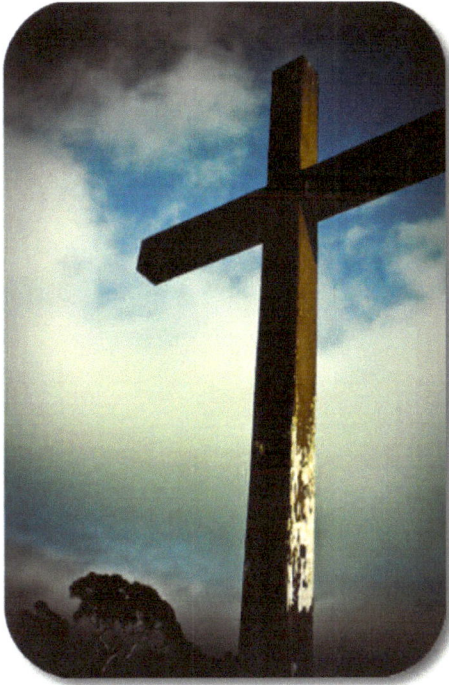

Luke 12:50
But I have a baptism to be baptized with, and how distressed I am till it is accomplished!

Jesus knew that He had come into the world to die for the sins of the world. Luke 12:50 is a clear indication that Jesus pointed towards another Baptism. At the time that Jesus made the statement of having "a *baptism to be baptized with*" He had already been baptized by John (Luke 3:21) and God had already filled Him with the Holy Spirit (Luke 3:22; Luke 4:1). Therefore it is evident that Jesus pointed towards another Baptism, which was His death, in which He confirmed to His disciples when he said, "*you will indeed drink the cup that I drink, and with the baptism that I am baptized with you will be baptized*" (Mark 10:39).

Romans 6:3-5
3 Or do you not know that as many of us as were baptized into Christ Jesus were baptized into His death? 4 Therefore we were buried with Him through baptism into death, that just as Christ was raised from the dead by the glory of the Father, even so we also should walk in newness of life. For if we have been united together in the likeness of His death, certainly we also shall be in the likeness of His resurrection,

The *Baptism into death* is what identifies the New Testament believer with the death and burial of Jesus Christ. This is a necessity and reality. When a new believer comes to faith in Jesus Christ he becomes a new creation and old things pass away (2 Cor 5:17) and since Christ is in him the body is dead because of sin (Rom 8:10). The new believer that has come to faith in Christ is now dead indeed to sin (Rom 6:11) being buried with Christ in baptism (Col 2:12). It is the fellowship of the suffering of Jesus Christ that conforms us to His death (Phi 3:10).

Why Should Believers Be Baptized?	
Because Jesus was baptized	**Matthew 3:13-16** Then Jesus came from Galilee to John at the Jordan to be baptized by him. 14 And John *tried* to prevent Him, saying, "I need to be baptized by You, and are You coming to me?" 15 But Jesus answered and said to him, "*Permit it to be so* now, for thus it is fitting for us to fulfill all righteousness." Then he allowed Him. 16 When He had been baptized, Jesus came up immediately from the water; and behold, the heavens were opened to Him, and He saw the Spirit of God descending like a dove and alighting upon Him.
Because Jesus Commanded it (The Great Commission)	**Matthew 28:19** Go therefore and make disciples of all the nations, baptizing them in the name of the Father and of the Son and of the Holy Spirit.
Because it is a rejection of the will of God not to be baptized	**Luke 7:30** But the Pharisees and lawyers rejected the will of God for themselves, not having been baptized by him.

Making Sense Of It All

Ephesians 4:5

There is one body and one Spirit, just as you were called in one hope of your calling; 5 one Lord, one faith, **one baptism**; 6 one God and Father of all, who *is* above all, and through all, and in you all.

As complex as the *Doctrine of Baptisms* might seem, it is actually quite simple. With all these different types of baptisms, one would have to try and figure out how to view them through the lens of Ephesians 4:5 which declares that there is *one Lord, one faith, one baptism*. How can we have the *Doctrine of Baptisms* but yet there be **one baptism**. To make sense of this we would have to go back to the basic definition of **Baptism** which is *the act of identifying one object with another*. Each one of these Baptisms performs this **one** act of identifying the believer with relationship with God.

Doctrine Of Baptisms		
Baptism	**Category**	**Relationship**
Circumcision of the heart	*A type of Baptism*	*Identifies the believer in Covenant Relationship with God*
Baptism into the Cloud & Sea	*A type of Baptism*	*Identified the Children of Israel with God through Moses*
Baptism of John	*A Baptism of Repentance*	*Identifies us in Covenant Relationship with God -* **Symbolic of His Death, Burial, & Resurrection**
Baptism of the Holy Spirit	*A Baptism of Power*	*Identifies us with Life in Christ*
Baptism into Death	*A type of Baptism*	*Identifies us with Death in Christ*

Just as there is one Lord who manifests Himself as Father, Son, And Holy Spirit, there is one baptism that identifies the Children of God in relationship with God which is manifested also in different ways. But a carnal mind cannot understand spiritual things. This is why Apostle Paul said that I speak to you in Human terms because of the weakness of your flesh (Romans 6:19). It is the Holy Spirit that guides us into all truth (John 16:13).

F.Y.I. – Did Jesus Baptize?

Look up the following passages and answer the corresponding questions

John 3:22-36; John 4:1&2; Mark 1:8

1. Did Jesus Baptize?

_____

_____

2. Why or Why Not?

_____

_____

1. Explain in detail what the word *Baptism* means.

   _____

   _____

2. Generally speaking, what is the focus of the Old Testament?

   _____

   _____

3. Generally speaking, what is the focus of the New Testament?

   _____

   _____

4. Explain in detail what is the Circumcision of the heart.

   _____

   _____

5. Explain in detail what is the *Baptism* into the Cloud & Sea.

   _____

   _____

6. Explain in detail what is the *Baptism* of John.

   _____

   _____

7. Explain in detail what is the *Baptism* of the Holy Spirit.

   _____

   _____

8. Explain in detail what is the *Baptism* into Death.

   _____

   _____

9. Explain in detail why a believer should be Baptized.

   _____

   _____

10. Explain in detail the unity of all of the *baptisms*.

    _____

    _____

Create an outline that highlights the content covered in this unit. Be sure to include scriptures & detail. Your outline should be able to serve as a roadmap for others.

_____
_____
_____
_____
_____
_____
_____
_____
_____
_____
_____
_____
_____
_____
_____
_____
_____
_____
_____
_____
_____
_____
_____
_____
_____
_____
_____
_____
_____
_____
_____
_____
_____

Laying on of Hands

Hebrews 6

1 Therefore, leaving the discussion of the elementary *principles* of Christ, let us go on to perfection, not laying again the foundation of *repentance from dead works* and of *faith toward God*, 2 of the *doctrine of baptisms*, of *laying on of hands*, of *resurrection of the dead*, and of *eternal judgment*.

Unit 4

Scan QR Code to watch video

FOUNDATION
THE ELEMENTARY TEACHINGS OF CHRISTIANITY

FOUNDATION
THE ELEMENTARY TEACHINGS OF CHRISTIANITY

Hebrews 6

1 Therefore, leaving the discussion of the elementary principles of Christ, let us go on to perfection, not laying again the foundation of *repentance from dead works* and of *faith toward God*, 2 of the *doctrine of baptisms*, of *laying on of hands*, of *resurrection of the dead*, and of *eternal judgment*.

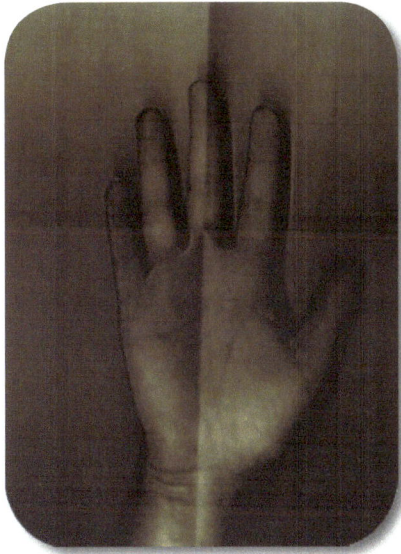

The Doctrine of the *Laying on of Hands* is one seldom referenced. The truths that this doctrine holds are paramount to the life of a Christian and essential in the spiritual growth and vitality of the Church. In general, the *Laying on of Hands* is a Biblical practice observed when a believer or group of believers lay their hands on someone to pray or to declare something. When this practice is not observed it will be evident. Evidence all through out scripture points to the necessity of the *Laying on of hands*.

What did Jesus say about *"The Laying on of Hands"*?

Mark 16:15-18

"Go into all the world and preach the gospel to every creature. He who believes and is baptized will be saved but he who does not believe will be condemned. And these signs will follow those who believe: In My name they will cast out demons; they will speak with new tongues; they will take up serpents; and if they drink anything deadly, it will by no means hurt them; they will lay hands on the sick, and they will recover."

The above passage is what has come to be known as the Great Commission which was given to the Church by Jesus before He ascended into Heaven. In this passage Jesus tells His disciples that "these signs will follow those who believe". Along with all of the other signs mentioned Jesus states "that those who believe will lay hands on the sick, and they will recover." For Jesus to mention this along with the Great Commission shows the importance of this type of work.

There are many applications of the Laying on of Hands that can be found throughout the scriptures. Listed below is a detailed chart that displays different passages in both the Old Testament and New Testament where the Laying on of hands can be observed.

Laying on of Hands			
Scripture	**Outcome**	**Scripture**	**Outcome**
Genesis 48:14-17	Blessings	Acts 19:6	Received the Holy Spirit
Numbers 27:18-23	inauguration/ordination	Matthew 9:23-26	The dead raised
Matthew 8:2-4	Cleansing/healing	Numbers 8:10-12	Transfer of sin
Matthew 20-32-34	Received Sight/healing	Acts 6:5,6	Ordination
Mark 6:4-6	Healings	Acts 13:1-3	Commissioned
Mark 7:31-37	Ears opened/ tongue loosed/ healing	Mark 10:13-16	Prayer of blessings
Mark 8:22- 25	Received sight/healing	Acts 5:12	Signs & Wonders
Luke 4:40-42	Healing/demonic deliverance	Acts 14:3	Signs & Wonders
Acts 9:10-17	Received sight/ Holy Spirit	1 Timothy 4:14	Impartation of Spiritual Gifts
Acts 28:8	Healing	2 Timothy 1:6	Impartation of Spiritual Gifts
Acts 8:14-19	Received the Holy Spirit	Mark 16:15-18	Recovery of the sick

These Biblical examples observed throughout the scriptures reveal many things about the *Laying on of Hands*. We see how the *Laying on of Hands* was used in blessings, ordinations, healing, miracles, and the giving of the Holy Spirit. If anything, the previous passages illustrate not just the literal applications of this doctrine but also the importance and the consistency of its observation throughout the scriptures.

What happens during *"the laying on of hands"*?

The Laying on of hands is not some mystical pagan practice but rather a Biblical practical truth. Most people, believers included, are so far removed from Biblical principles that the *Laying on of Hands* seems foreign to their tradition. Although misunderstood, what truly happens during the *Laying on of Hands* is an impartation.

Word Check: *Impartation*

This word impartation generally means to communicate information, knowledge, or substance from one to another. In a more specific viewpoint it means to give something or someone a particular quality. To impart simply means to transfer.

To understand the simple principles of impartation lets use for an example a cellular phone. When a cell phone is need of a charge one would simply plug it into the charger, which would obviously be plugged in to some source of power. Technically, what happens is that the power, which is coming from the source of power, is transferred through the cable that connects the phone to the power source. The cable is therefore serving as a conduit or a channel which transfers the power from the source to the cellular phone. The end result is that the cellular phone has received an impartation or a transfer of power from the source of power through the cable. This basic principle can be seen in the following passage:

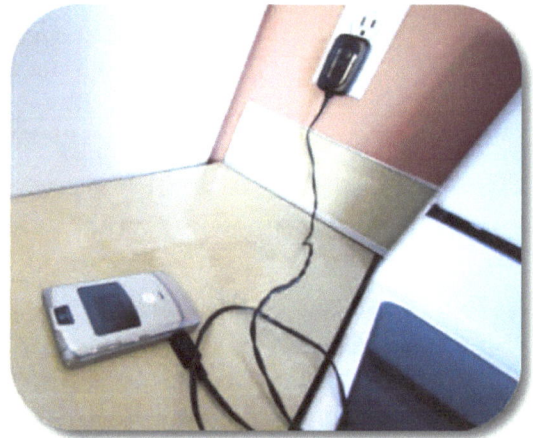

Luke 8:43-46
Now a woman, having a flow of blood for twelve years, who had spent all her livelihood on physicians and could not be healed by any, 44 came from behind and touched the border of His garment. And immediately her flow of blood stopped. 45 And Jesus said, "Who touched Me?" When all denied it, Peter and those with him said, "Master, the multitudes throng and press You, and You say, 'Who touched Me?'" 46 But Jesus said, "Somebody touched Me, for *I perceived power going out from Me.*"

In the above passage we observe a woman whom in having an incurable flow of blood for twelve years came into contact with Jesus. This woman had made up in her mind that if she could just touch the border of His garment that she would be healed. The passage goes on to tell us that as she came from behind and touched His garment that immediately her flow of blood stopped and at that moment Jesus said, "Who touched me". His disciples responded by saying "Master, the multitudes throng and press You and You say, "Who touched Me"". The question posed by His disciples is how could Jesus ask who touched Him when so many people were obviously pressing against Him as He walked through the multitudes? Jesus responded by saying, "Somebody touched Me, for I perceived power going out from Me". Jesus is literally saying that a transfer of power or an impartation had just taken place. Power had gone out from the Source which was Jesus when the woman touched Him. This principle can also be seen in the following passage.

Luke 6:17-19

And He came down with them and stood on a level place with a crowd of His disciples and a great multitude of people from all Judea and Jerusalem, and from the seacoast of Tyre and Sidon, who came to hear Him and be healed of their diseases, 18 as well as those who were tormented with unclean spirits. And they were healed. 19 And the whole multitude sought to touch Him, for power went out from Him and healed *them* all.

In the previous passage we can observe an impartation or a transfer of power. Jesus is standing in the midst of His disciples and a multitude of people who had come to hear Him and be healed. Verse 19 tells us that "*the whole multitude sought to touch Him*". The magnificent part is that this verse goes on to tell us that "*power went out from Him (Jesus) and healed them all*". In this passage, just as the previous one, we observe power transferring from the Source (Jesus) to the people and numerous healings taking place.

The objective of the two previous passages was to illustrate and make visible the transfer of power. Using this same principle let us now examine the following passage:

Acts 8:14-19

Now when the apostles who were at Jerusalem heard that Samaria had received the word of God, they sent Peter and John to them, 15 who, when they had come down, prayed for them that they might receive the Holy Spirit. 16 For as yet He had fallen upon none of them. They had only been baptized in the name of the Lord Jesus. 17 Then they laid hands on them, and they received the Holy Spirit. 18 And when Simon saw that through the laying on of the apostles' hands the Holy Spirit was given, he offered them money, 19 saying, "Give me this power also, that anyone on whom I lay hands may receive the Holy Spirit."

In this passage we observe the *Laying on of Hands* powerfully at work. Phillip had preached Christ to the city of Samaria and they had received the Word of God and were baptized. When this news spread to the Apostles who were at Jerusalem "*they sent Peter and John to them, who, when they had come down, prayed for them that they might receive the Holy Spirit*". The passage continues on to tell us that when Peter and John had laid hands on them that they received the Holy Spirit. This is one of the most beautiful applications of the *Laying on of Hands*. The observation was so obvious that when Simon, who had once been a sorcerer in the city of Samaria, "*saw that through the laying on of the apostles' hands the Holy Spirit was given, he offered them money, saying, "Give me this power also, that anyone on whom I lay hands may receive the Holy Spirit."* This was obviously a real experience that Simon had witnessed that stirred him to try and purchase this power that the Apostles had seemingly had in the *Laying on of Hands*.

When should "*the laying on of hands*" not be practiced in the Church?

To begin with, the *Laying on of Hands* should only be performed by those who are mature and rooted in the faith. One does not become a Christian on one day and begin laying hands on people the next day. There should be progressive evidence of spiritual growth in a believer's life and a level of discernment. The Apostle Paul tells Timothy to "*not lay hands on anyone hastily*" or quickly. This would be in situations like deliverance or casting out demons. There has to be a level of discernment and it has to be led by the Holy Spirit. There must be a discipline of fasting and praying in the believers' life just as Jesus taught His disciples (Mt 17:21). If not, the believer would find himself vulnerable to fall prey to the same attack as the one whom he is laying hands on. One must remember that spirits have the capability of transferring and causing both spiritual and physical harm (Acts 19:16).

The Power of Hands
A Powerful Short Film

Scan QR Code
to watch video

1. What did Jesus say about the *Laying on of Hands* in the Great Commission?

    _____

    _____

2. List several occasions where the *Laying on of Hands* would be practiced.

    _____

    _____

3. What happens during the *Laying on of Hands*?

    _____

    _____

4. In your own words give an example of impartation.

    _____

    _____

5. In Luke 8:43-46 how did Jesus know that someone had touched Him?

    _____

    _____

6. In Luke 6:17-19 what healed the multitude of people who sought to touch Jesus?

    _____

    _____

7. In Acts 8:14-19 how did the people of Samaria receive the Holy Spirit?

    _____

    _____

8. Why did Simon offer the Apostles money?

    _____

    _____

9. When should the *Laying on of Hands* not be practiced?

    _____

    _____

10. Why is the *Laying on of Hands* so important to the Church?

    _____

    _____

Create an outline that highlights the content covered in this unit. Be sure to include scriptures & detail. Your outline should be able to serve as a roadmap for others.

Resurrection of the Dead

Hebrews 6

1 Therefore, leaving the discussion of the elementary *principles* of Christ, let us go on to perfection, not laying again the foundation of *repentance from dead works* and of *faith toward God*, 2 of the *doctrine of baptisms*, of *laying on of hands*, of *resurrection of the dead*, and of *eternal judgment*.

Unit 5

FOUNDATION

THE ELEMENTARY TEACHINGS OF CHRISTIANITY

FOUNDATION

THE ELEMENTARY TEACHINGS OF CHRISTIANITY

Hebrews 6
1 Therefore, leaving the discussion of the elementary principles of Christ, let us go on to perfection, not laying again the foundation of *repentance from dead works* and of *faith toward God*, 2 of the *doctrine of baptisms*, of *laying on of hands*, of *resurrection of the dead*, and of *eternal judgment*.

Ever since the fall of man in the Garden of Eden, mankind, who was created to be an eternal being, has been subject to death. When sin entered into the world through Adam's disobedience it (sin) became a gateway for death to enter also and spread to all men (Rom 5:12). For this reason man stands in need of a savior. This is the premise that the doctrine of the *Resurrection of the Dead* is built upon, which is the hope that man would be raised from death to eternal life. This doctrine is both fundamental to the faith and the message of the Gospel.

Word Check: *Resurrection*

The word translated most often as Resurrection in the New Testament comes from the Greek word *Anastasis*. This word literally means a raising up or rising. It speaks towards a bodily rising of the dead from death to life.[ix]

Word Check: *Resuscitation*

Resuscitation is a common English word that holds similar but however distinct implications. This word points to the reviving of someone from unconsciousness or apparent death.[x]

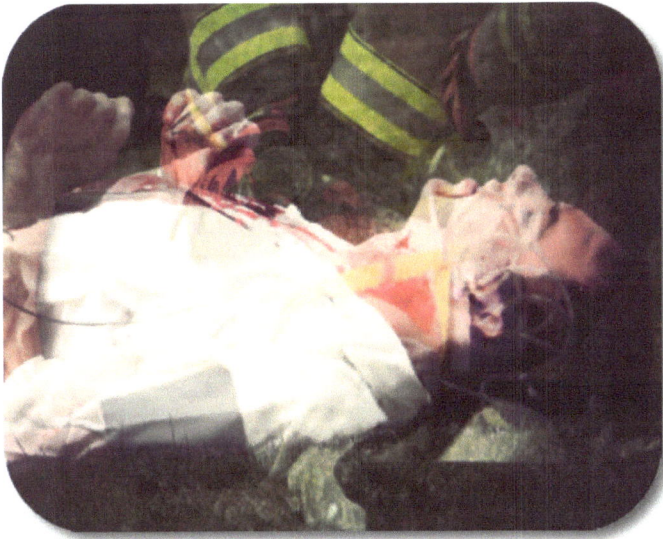

Resurrection vs. Resuscitation

The word *Resurrection* points towards the transition from death into Eternity. Those resurrected will partake in eternal life.

The word *Resuscitation* points towards a restoration to earthly life. Those resuscitated, however, will eventually die again to await the Resurrection.

The word resurrection is also used to point towards the event when believers are transitioned to a new state of being at the time when the dead are raised. This is the hope that all those of the faith anticipate.

Old Testament

The doctrine of *Resurrection of the Dead* had not fully been revealed in the Old Testament, however the hope and the foundation for what was to come had been laid. Old Testament believers just like New Testament believers had an eager expectation that their bodies would one day rise after death. We can see the foundation of this doctrine being poured in the following passages:

Daniel 12:2
Multitudes who sleep in the dust of the earth will awake: some to everlasting life, others to shame and everlasting contempt.

Isaiah 25:8
he will swallow up death forever.

Isaiah 26:19
But your dead will live; their bodies will rise. You who dwell in the dust, wake up and shout for joy. Your dew is like the dew of the morning; the earth will give birth to her dead.

The lives of Enoch and Elijah, who were both Old Testament believers, indisputably pointed towards a life that succeeds this earthly life. Enoch was the seventh from Adam and the great-grandfather of Noah (Gen 5:18-24). The Bible tells us that Enoch walked with God and God took him and that he did not see death (Heb 11:5). The same can be found with Elijah. God took him up to heaven in a whirlwind in the presence of Elisha. These two stories not only gave hope to Old Testament believers but also gives authority to an event known as The Rapture which will be discussed later.

But still there was so much mystery surrounding the *Resurrection of the Dead* during the time of the Old Testament. This can even be seen in the Gospels when the Sadducees, who were part of the religious community at the time of Christ, whom themselves did not believe in the resurrection (Matthew 22:23). In fact, they went as far as attempting to challenge Jesus by questioning Him regarding the resurrection (Matthew 22:23-33).

Abraham's Bosom

One question that often arises is where did the spirits of believers that died before the time of Jesus go after they departed? It's not clear if the believers of that day knew the absolute answer to that question. Although there was a hope and a Biblical foundation to support life after death, as said earlier the revelation of the details remained vague. However, careful study of the scriptures gives a clear implication to this answer. In the Gospel of Luke we find Jesus speaking on this very notion in the story of the *Rich Man & Lazarus*.

Luke 16:19-31
19 "There was a certain rich man who was clothed in purple and fine linen and fared sumptuously every day. 20 But there was a certain beggar named Lazarus, full of sores, who was laid at his gate, 21 desiring to be fed with the crumbs which fell from the rich man's table. Moreover the dogs came and licked his sores. 22 So it was that the beggar died, and was carried by the angels to Abraham's bosom. The rich man also died and was buried. 23 And being in torments in Hades, he lifted up his eyes and saw Abraham afar off, and Lazarus in his bosom. 24 "Then he cried and said, 'Father Abraham, have mercy on me, and send Lazarus that he may dip the tip of his finger in water and cool my tongue; for I am tormented in this flame.' 25 But Abraham said, 'Son, remember that in your lifetime you received your good things, and likewise Lazarus evil things; but now he is comforted and you are tormented. 26 And besides all this, between us and you there is a great gulf fixed, so that those who want to pass from here to you cannot, nor can those from there pass to us.' 27 "Then he said, 'I beg you therefore, father, that you would send him to my father's house, 28 for I have five brothers, that he may testify to them, lest they also come to this place of torment.' 29 Abraham said to him, 'They have Moses and the prophets; let them hear them.' 30 And he said, 'No, father Abraham; but if one goes to them from the dead, they will repent.' 31 But he said to him, 'If they do not hear Moses and the prophets, neither will they be persuaded though one rise from the dead.'"

In this passage Jesus mentions a place referred to as *Abrahams Bosom*. He describes it as a place where the angels carried Lazarus. Interesting enough is that this place known as *Abrahams Bosom* was visible from Hades, which is the Greek word for hell, only to be separated by "a great gulf fixed", which can also be translated as an established gaping opening. Nowhere else in the scriptures do we find the term *Abrahams Bosom* used, however, ancient Jewish customs holds this to be a place where the righteous dead awaited judgment.

The Old Testament had many passages that pointed towards this, which are easier to identify looking backwards from a New Testament believers' point of view than looking forward from an Old Testament believers' point of view.

Psalm 16:10
For You will not leave my soul in *Sheol*, Nor will You allow Your Holy One to see corruption.

Psalm 86:13
For great is Your mercy toward me, And You have delivered my soul from the depths of *Sheol*.

Word Check: *Hades*

Hades is the Greek word used in the New Testament that is sometimes translated into the word Hell or grave. Hades was considered to be the realm of the dead.[xi]

Word Check: *Sheol*

Sheol is the Hebrew word used in the Old Testament that is sometimes translated in the word Hell, grave, or pit. Sheol was considered to be the underworld or place of the dead.[xii]

The Hebrew word Sheol in the Old Testament is the same word used for Hell, which speaks of the same location represented by the word Hades in the New Testament. From the previous scriptures one can see the hope illustrated in the Old Testament that God would not leave their soul in Sheol, but deliver them. Even today the word *Hell* is not fully understood by most modern day believers because of the lack of Old Testament understanding. The concept of Hell as a place will be explored in more detail in the following chapter.

Abrahams Bosom was a place where believers before the time of Christ went after they died. Abraham as a Biblical figure was considered to be the father of all of us in the faith (Romans 4:16). It was to him that God made the covenant of our faith in the Old Testament (Genesis 17). This is why Jesus referred to this place as *Abrahams Bosom*. The scriptures teach us that when Jesus died he went down to Hades, set the captives free, preached (proclaimed) to the prisoners, and was resurrected on the third day. The following scriptures declare His works

Acts 2:22-31
"Men of Israel, hear these words: Jesus of Nazareth, a Man attested by God to you by miracles, wonders, and signs which God did through Him in your midst, as you yourselves also know— 23 Him, being delivered by the determined purpose and foreknowledge of God, you have taken[a] by lawless hands, have crucified, and put to death; 24 whom God raised up, having loosed the pains of death, because it was not possible that He should be held by it. 25 For David says concerning Him:
  ' I foresaw the LORD always before my face,
  For He is at my right hand, that I may not be shaken.
  26 Therefore my heart rejoiced, and my tongue was glad;
  Moreover my flesh also will rest in hope.
  27 For You will not leave my soul in Hades,
  Nor will You allow Your Holy One to see corruption.
  28 You have made known to me the ways of life;
  You will make me full of joy in Your presence.'
29 "Men and brethren, let me speak freely to you of the patriarch David, that he is both dead and buried, and his tomb is with us to this day. 30 Therefore, being a prophet, and knowing that God had sworn with an oath to him that of the fruit of his body, according to the flesh, He would raise up the Christ to sit on his throne, 31 he, foreseeing this, spoke concerning the resurrection of the Christ, that His soul was not left in Hades, nor did His flesh see corruption.

Ephesians 4:8-11
Therefore He says: "*When He ascended on high, He led captivity captive, And gave gifts to men.*" 9 (Now this, "*He ascended*" — what does it mean but that He also first descended into the lower parts of the earth? 10 He who descended is also the One who ascended far above all the heavens, that He might fill all things.)

1 Peter 3:18-20
For Christ also suffered once for sins, the just for the unjust, that He might bring us to God, being put to death in the flesh but made alive by the Spirit, 19 by whom also He went and preached to the spirits in prison, 20 who formerly were disobedient, when once the Divine longsuffering waited in the days of Noah, while *the* ark was being prepared, in which a few, that is, eight souls, were saved through water.

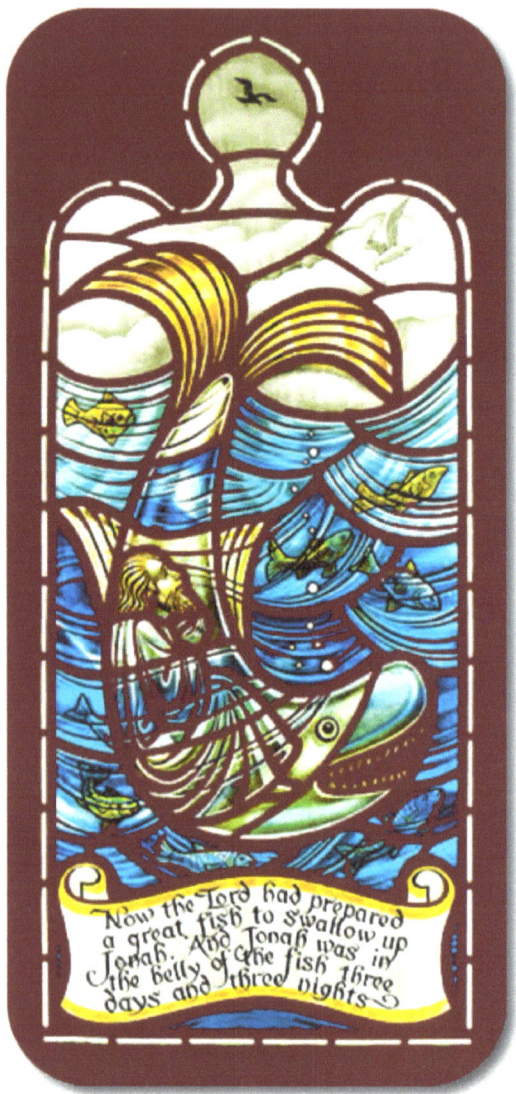

Another clear implication to this can be found in the Gospels during one of the accounts that Jesus had with the Scribes and Pharisees in which they challenged Him to show them a sign. Jesus replies swiftly to their request prophesying to them of what was to come as it regards to His death, burial, and resurrection.

Luke 12:39,40
But He answered and said to them, "An evil and adulterous generation seeks after a sign, and no sign will be given to it except the sign of the prophet Jonah. 40 For as Jonah was three days and three nights in the belly of the great fish, so will the Son of Man be three days and three nights in the heart of the earth.

Jesus Himself gives the interpretation of His own statement by telling the Scribes and Pharisees that He was to be three days in the heart of the earth just as Jonah spent three days in the belly of the great fish. All of those educated in the Old Testament scriptures would have understood what He was saying. To understand this statement one must first understand that when Jonah was swallowed up by the whale, that he died as he says his "soul fainted", but afterwards the Lord brought up his life from the "pit", which is a reference for Sheol as seen in the following passage.

Jonah 2:6,7
I went down to the moorings of the mountains; The earth with its bars *closed* behind me forever; Yet You have brought up my life from the pit, O LORD, my God. 7 "When my soul fainted within me, I remembered the LORD; And my prayer went *up* to You, Into Your holy temple.

The Ressurection of Christ

The *Resurrection of Christ* is the keystone of the Christian faith. This historic act in which God raised Jesus' body from the dead three days after His death on the cross is the hope that all believers rest securely in. The testimony of this account can be found in all four of the Gospels.

Matthew 28:6
He is not here; for He is **risen**, as He said. Come, see the place where the Lord lay.

Mark 16:6
But he said to them, "Do not be alarmed. You seek Jesus of Nazareth, who was crucified. He is **risen**! He is not here. See the place where they laid Him.

Luke 24:6
He is not here, but is **risen**! Remember how He spoke to you when He was still in Galilee,

John 2:22
Therefore, when He had **risen** from the dead, His disciples remembered that He had said this to them; and they believed the Scripture and the word which Jesus had said.

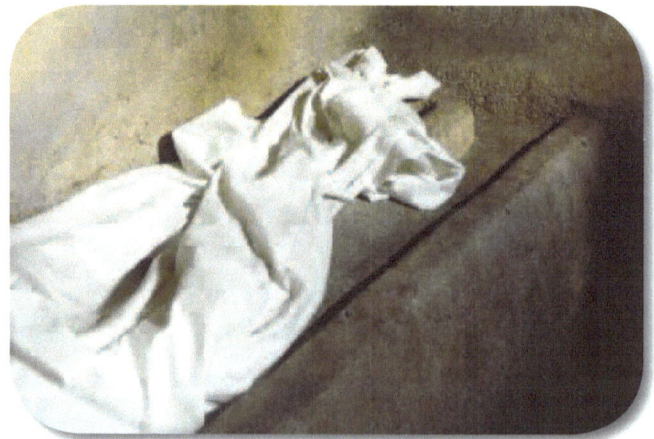

After His resurrection Jesus presented Himself alive to His disciples for forty days (Acts 1:3) even allowing Thomas to examine the wounds in His hands and His side from the crucifixion (John 20:27) in the midst of the other disciples. He spoke to them about things pertaining to the Kingdom of God (Acts 1:3). After Jesus ascended back to Heaven (Acts 1:9), the testimony of His death, burial, and resurrection became the main message of those who followed Him. This can clearly be seen on the day of Pentecost, which is the day the Holy Spirit was given to the Church. On this day Peter stood up before the people and proclaimed the message of the death, burial, and resurrection of Jesus Christ.

Acts 2:22-24
22 "Men of Israel, hear these words: Jesus of Nazareth, a Man attested by God to you by miracles, wonders, and signs which God did through Him in your midst, as you yourselves also know— 23 Him, being delivered by the determined purpose and foreknowledge of God, you have take by lawless hands, have crucified, and put to death; 24 whom God raised up, having loosed the pains of death, because it was not possible that He should be held by it.

Apostle Paul who wrote most of the epistles (letters) of the New Testament made no excuses for the message of the resurrected Jesus Christ. This message was the focal point of all of his writings to the Churches and his ministry. Some mocked this message (Acts 17:32). Paul placed the entire faith on the resurrection of Christ, understanding that this was the most important event in the history of mankind.

I Cor 15:12-18 (Christ Risen)
12 Now if Christ is preached that He has been raised from the dead, how do some among you say that there is no resurrection of the dead? 13 But if there is no resurrection of the dead, then Christ is not risen. 14 And if Christ is not risen, then our preaching is empty and your faith is also empty. 15 Yes, and we are found false witnesses of God, because we have testified of God that He raised up Christ, whom He did not raise up—if in fact the dead do not rise. 16 For if *the* dead do not rise, then Christ is not risen. 17 And if Christ is not risen, your faith is futile; you are still in your sins! 18 Then also those who have fallen asleep in Christ have perished. 19 If in this life only we have hope in Christ, we are of all men the most pitiable.

Acts 24:21
unless it is for this one statement which I cried out, standing among them, 'Concerning the resurrection of the dead I am being judged by you this day.'"

The message of the Resurrection of Christ is the central theme of the scriptures. This is the message that every minister of the Gospel has proclaimed since the time of Christ. This is what a large portion of Old Testament prophecies pointed towards. This is the testimony that so many believers have been willing to lay down their lives for.

New Testament (Ressurection of the Believer)

Ever since Christ ascended into Heaven, those who follow Him have earnestly been awaiting His return and the event known to many as *The Resurrection*. This is the event in which those who have placed their faith in the God of the Bible will be transitioned from the state of death to eternal life. At this time all of the physical bodies of those who have died in the faith will be raised in incorruption (I Corinthians 15:42,43,44). These bodies will be immortal in nature, a true spiritual body also referred to as a *Glorified Body*. The following passages speak of the resurrection.

1 Thessalonians 4:13-17

13 But I do not want you to be ignorant, brethren, concerning those who have fallen asleep, lest you sorrow as others who have no hope. 14 For if we believe that Jesus died and rose again, even so God will bring with Him those who sleep in Jesus. 15 For this we say to you by the word of the Lord, that we who are alive *and* remain until the coming of the Lord will by no means precede those who are asleep. 16 For the Lord Himself will descend from heaven with a shout, with the voice of an archangel, and with the trumpet of God. And the dead in Christ will rise first. 17 Then we who are alive *and* remain shall be caught up together with them in the clouds to meet the Lord in the air. And thus we shall always be with the Lord.

I Corinthians 15:35-54

35 But someone will say, "How are the dead raised up? And with what body do they come?" 36 Foolish one, what you sow is not made alive unless it dies. 37 And what you sow, you do not sow that body that shall be, but mere grain— perhaps wheat or some other *grain*. 38 But God gives it a body as He pleases, and to each seed its own body. 39 All flesh *is* not the same flesh, but *there is* one *kind* of flesh of men, another flesh of animals, another of fish, *and* another of birds. 40 *There are* also celestial bodies and terrestrial bodies; but the glory of the celestial *is* one, and the *glory* of the terrestrial is another. 41 *There is* one glory of the sun, another glory of the moon, and another glory of the stars; for one star differs from *another* star in glory. 42 So also is the resurrection of the dead. *The body* is sown in corruption, it is raised in incorruption. 43 It is sown in dishonor, it is raised in glory. It is sown in weakness, it is raised in power. 44 It is sown a natural body, it is raised a spiritual body. There is a natural body, and there is a spiritual body. 45 And so it is written, "*The first man Adam became a living being*." The last Adam became a life-giving spirit. 46 However, the spiritual is not first, but the natural, and afterward the spiritual. 47 The first man was of the earth, *made* of dust; the second Man *is* the Lord from heaven. 48 As *was* the *man* of dust, so also *are* those *who are made* of dust; and as *is* the heavenly *Man*, so also *are* those *who are* heavenly. 49 And as we have borne the image of the *man* of dust, we shall also bear the image of the heavenly *Man*. 50 Now this I say, brethren, that flesh and blood cannot inherit the kingdom of God; nor does corruption inherit incorruption. 51 Behold, I tell you a mystery: We shall not all sleep, but we shall all be changed— 52 in a moment, in the twinkling of an eye, at the last trumpet. For the trumpet will sound, and the dead will be raised incorruptible, and we shall be changed. 53 For this corruptible must put on incorruption, and this mortal *must* put on immortality. 54 So when this corruptible has put on incorruption, and this mortal has put on immortality, then shall be brought to pass the saying that is written: "*Death is swallowed up in victory*."

New Testament (The Rapture)

The Resurrection as it is said is the day that Christ will come back for His Church. Not only those who are dead, but also those "who are alive and remain shall be caught up together with them in the clouds to meet the Lord in the air" (1 Thessalonians 4:17). This is often referred to as *The Rapture*.

Word Check: *Rapture*

The word "rapture" comes from the Latin *rapere* used by the Vulgate (early 5th-century Latin version of the Bible) to translate the Greek word *harpaz*, which is rendered by the phrase "caught up" in most English translations.[xiii] The Greek word *harpaz* can also be translated as "catch away", "pluck", "take by force", or "pull".[xiv]

The Rapture is part of what is called end time prophecy or what is formally known as Eschatology (the study of end times). There were those in the time of the early church who had feared that this event had already taken place and that they had been left behind. Apostle Paul felt it necessary to comfort such worries in his second letter written to the church of Thessalonica.

2 Thessalonians 2:1-7
Now, brethren, concerning the coming of our Lord Jesus Christ and our gathering together to Him, we ask you, 2 not to be soon shaken in mind or troubled, either by spirit or by word or by letter, as if from us, as though the day of Christ had come. 3 Let no one deceive you by any means; for that *Day will not come* unless the falling away comes first, and the man of sin is revealed, the son of perdition, 4 who opposes and exalts himself above all that is called God or that is worshiped, so that he sits as God in the temple of God, showing himself that he is God.5 Do you not remember that when I was still with you I told you these things? 6 And now you know what is restraining, that he may be revealed in his own time. 7 For the mystery of lawlessness is already at work; only He who now restrains *will do so* until He is taken out of the way.

Jesus even revealed this event in His teachings when His disciples came to Him privately on the Mount of Olives and asked Him what would be the signs of His coming and the end of the age (Matthew 24:3). In great detail, Jesus told them of things which were to come. In the following passage Jesus speaks to His disciples on how "one will be taken and the other left".

Matthew 24:36-41
"But of that day and hour no one knows, not even the angels of heaven, but My Father only. 37 But as the days of Noah *were*, so also will the coming of the Son of Man be. 38 For as in the days before the flood, they were eating and drinking, marrying and giving in marriage, until the day that Noah entered the ark, 39 and did not know until the flood came and took them all away, so also will the coming of the Son of Man be. 40 Then two *men* will be in the field: one will be taken and the other left. 41 Two *women will* be grinding at the mill: one will be taken and the other left.

The Rapture and *The Resurrection* go hand and hand due to the fact that this is the same event. While *The Rapture* refers to those who are alive at the time of Christ return who will be caught up in the air (1 Thessalonians 4:17), *The Resurrection* refers to those who are dead and in Christ whose bodies will be raised (1 Thessalonians 4:16) from death to incorruptible (1 Corinthians 15:52). Just as Paul explained, first the dead in Christ will rise, then those "who are alive *and* remain shall be caught up together with them in the clouds to meet the Lord in the air" (1 Thessalonians 4:17). This must be understood in the context of this being the first resurrection, which takes place during the time of His second appearance (Heb 9:28).

The Resurrection of the Dead as stated earlier is fundamental to the faith. The risen Christ is the first-fruits of those who will rise at His return (1 Corinthians 15:23) which are all believers. However the rest of the dead shall also rise in what is called the second resurrection, which takes place over a thousand years later.

Acts 24:15
I have hope in God, which they themselves also accept, that there will be a resurrection of the dead, both of the just and the unjust.

Revelation 20:5,6
But the rest of the dead did not live again until the thousand years were finished. This is the first resurrection. 6 Blessed and holy is he who has part in the first resurrection. Over such the second death has no power, but they shall be priests of God and of Christ, and shall reign with Him a thousand years.

Scripture clearly teaches that there will be two resurrections. The first resurrection which is the same event as the rapture will take place when Jesus returns for His Church in the clouds (1 Thessalonians 4:17) and the second resurrection will take place after Satan is destroyed (Revelation 20:7-14). One of the clearest depictions of this truth can be found in the Gospels as Jesus is proclaiming His authority to the Jews.

John 5:28,29
28 Do not marvel at this; for the hour is coming in which all who are in the graves will hear His voice 29 and come forth—those who have done good, to the resurrection of life, and those who have done evil, to the resurrection of condemnation.

As it pertains to *The Resurrections* and its power and everything that it is from the hope to the anticipation, Jesus spoke these powerful words in the Gospel of John: "*I am the resurrection*".

John 11:25
Jesus said to her, "I am the resurrection and the life. He who believes in Me, though he may die, he shall live.

1. What is the difference between the word *Resurrection* and *Resuscitation*?

   _____

   _____

2. What was significant about the lives of Enoch and Elijah?

   _____

   _____

3. Where did believers before the time of Jesus go after death?

   _____

   _____

4. What separated the place of the just and the unjust in death?

   _____

   _____

5. What took place between the time Jesus died on the cross and His resurrection?

   _____

   _____

6. What did Jesus allow Thomas to do and why?

   _____

   _____

7. What is the central message of the New Testament writings?

   _____

   _____

8. What does the Bible declare will happen to the dead during the time of Christ's return?

   _____

   _____

9. What fears did Paul comfort the Church of Thessalonica on?

   _____

   _____

10. How many resurrections does the Bible declare and how do they differ?

   _____

   _____

Create an outline that highlights the content covered in this unit. Be sure to include scriptures & detail. Your outline should be able to serve as a roadmap for others.

_____
_____
_____
_____
_____
_____
_____
_____
_____
_____
_____
_____
_____
_____
_____
_____
_____
_____
_____
_____
_____
_____
_____
_____
_____
_____
_____
_____
_____
_____
_____
_____

Eternal Judgment

Hebrews 6

1 Therefore, leaving the discussion of the elementary *principles* of Christ, let us go on to perfection, not laying again the foundation of *repentance from dead works* and of *faith toward God*, 2 of the *doctrine of baptisms*, of *laying on of hands*, of *resurrection of the dead*, and of *eternal judgment*.

Unit 6

Scan QR Code to watch video

FOUNDATION
THE ELEMENTARY TEACHINGS OF CHRISTIANITY

Hebrews 6

1 Therefore, leaving the discussion of the elementary *principles* of Christ, let us go on to perfection, not laying again the foundation of *repentance from dead works* and of *faith toward God*, 2 of the *doctrine of baptisms*, of *laying on of hands*, of *resurrection of the dead*, and of *eternal judgment*.

Eternal Judgment is an extremely significant doctrine necessary for a solid foundation of a believer. To understand this doctrine we must first look at the fundamental concept that is being expressed. The word judgment in this context is a judicial term that implies a judge, a decision or sentence, and a person receiving the judgment.

Word Check: *Judgment*

The word "*judgment*" used in this passage comes from the Greek word *Krima*, which literally means the punishment with which one is sentenced. This word is also translated elsewhere in the New Testament as damnation, condemnation, be condemned, go to law, and avenged.[xv]

In *Eternal Judgment* God decides a person's reward or punishment and this verdict is legally binding for eternity. There is no way around this judgment and there is no legal appeal to His verdict. The judgment of God is just (Psalms 7:11) and perfect and beyond reproach. To fully grasp this doctrine we will examine the procedure of judgment and how it applies to the grand scheme of the scriptures.

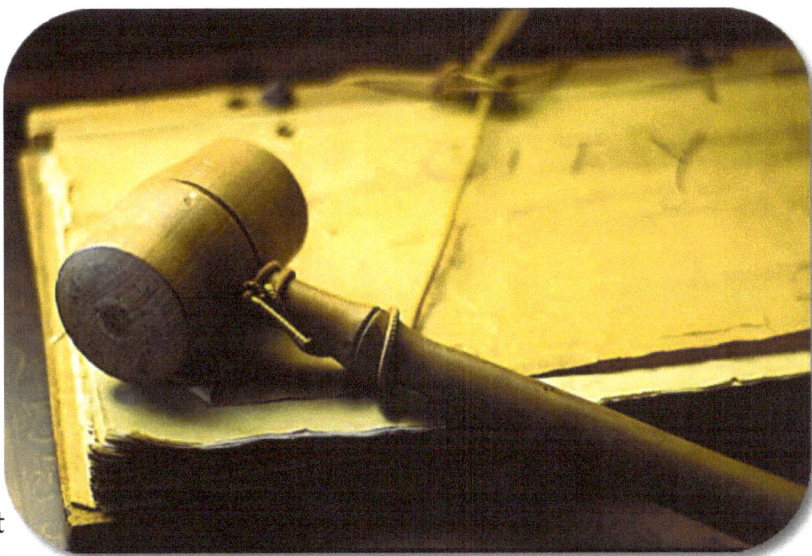

Who Is The Judge?

In any courtroom there is a judge that maintains order and holds the authority to convict, sentence, or perform any lawful action upon the defendant. The judge is an appointed figure sent forth to carry out the judiciary matters of a government. This same judiciary concept of a courtroom and a judge can be found all throughout the Bible. The scriptures reveal to us that Jesus has been appointed Judge of the living and the dead.

John 5:22

For the Father judges no one, but has committed all judgment to the Son,

Acts 10:42

And He commanded us to preach to the people, and to testify that it is He who was ordained by God to be Judge of the living and the dead.

Acts 17:31

because He has appointed a day on which He will judge the world in righteousness by the Man whom He has ordained. He has given assurance of this to all by raising Him from the dead."

Romans 2:16

in the day when God will judge the secrets of men by Jesus Christ, according to my gospel.

2 Corinthians 5:10

For we must all appear before the judgment seat of Christ

The expression "judgment seat" used in this passage comes from the Greek word *Bema*. This word is defined as a raised place mounted by steps which serves as the official seat of a judge. This word is also translated in the New Testament as Throne in some places.[xvi]

The Judgment Of Mankind

2 Corinthians 5:10

For *we must all appear before the judgment seat of Christ*, that each one may receive the things *done* in the body, according to what he has done, whether good or bad.

Paul uses the word *Bema* (2 Corinthians 5:10) to illustrate to the reader the realism of this unavoidable judgment that we must all face as he declares that "we must all appear before the judgment seat of Christ". He then goes on to tell us that mankind will be judged for what they have done in the body whether good or bad. This is a clear declaration of *Eternal Judgment*.

Hebrews 9:27, 28

And as it is appointed for men to die once, but after this the judgment, 28 so Christ was offered once to bear the sins of many. To those who eagerly wait for Him He will appear a second time, apart from sin, for salvation.

1 Peter 4:17

For the time has come for judgment to begin at the house of God; and if it begins with us first, what will be the end of those who do not obey the gospel of God?

For those who have accepted Christ as their Savior, the Bible declares Judgment has begun (1 Peter 4:17). This is yet a hard statement to understand but however a reality. The believer and the unbeliever are subject to two separate Judgments, two separate resurrections. For those who have received Salvation, they will be caught up in the clouds to meet the Lord when He appears (1 Thessalonians 4:17; Hebrews 9:28) which is referred to as the first resurrection or His second appearing.

Revelation 20:6

Blessed and holy is he who has part in the first resurrection.

The second resurrection is what is known as the *Great White Throne Judgment*. This is the judgment for those who were not a part of the first resurrection. Jesus explains this in great detail in the following passage.

John 5:24-30

"Most assuredly, I say to you, he who hears My word and believes in Him who sent Me has everlasting life, and shall not come into judgment, but has passed from death into life. 25 Most assuredly, I say to you, the hour is coming, and now is, when the dead will hear the voice of the Son of God; and those who hear will live. 26 For as the Father has life in Himself, so He has granted the Son to have life in Himself, 27 and has given Him authority to execute judgment also, because He is the Son of Man. 28 Do not marvel at this; for the hour is coming in which all who are in the graves will hear His voice 29 and come forth—those who have done good, to the resurrection of life, and those who have done evil, to the resurrection of condemnation. 30 I can of Myself do nothing. As I hear, I judge; and My judgment is righteous, because I do not seek My own will but the will of the Father who sent Me.

Those who have truly received salvation will not be subject to the *resurrection of condemnation* but their judgment or sentence will be LIFE in which Jesus spoke of as the *resurrection of life* (John 5:29). This is why the scriptures tell us that the time has come for judgment to begin at the house of God (1 Peter 4:17). The believer and unbeliever will not participate in the same judgment. Those who hold the gift of Salvation are being judged now. As for those who have done evil and have not repented unto Salvation, their judgment will be a frightening one of condemnation.

The word used for *judgment* in John 5:29 is translated into damnation in the King James Bible. This word comes from the Greek word *Krisis* meaning a sentence of condemnation, damnatory judgment, or condemnation and punishment.[xvii]

What Will God Judge?

Sin is what must be judged. The Bible teaches us that our iniquities separate us from God and our sins cause Him to hide His face from us (Isaiah 59:2). Since the fall of mankind in the Garden sin has dwelt in the flesh of man like a virus corrupting the moral clarity of creation for ages. Sin is made manifest in our hearts, our desires, our words, and our works and it is by these that man will be judged.

Ecclesiastes 12:14
For God will bring every work into judgment, Including every secret thing, Whether good or evil.

Matthew 12:36
But I say to you that for every idle word men may speak, they will give account of it in the day of judgment.

1 Corinthians 4:5
Therefore judge nothing before the time, until the Lord comes, who will both bring to light the hidden things of darkness and reveal the counsels of the hearts. Then each one's praise will come from God.

What Is The Standard Of Judgment?

In most courtrooms the standard of judgment is based on an interpretation of laws and documents. For example, in the United States of America, every citizen has a constitutional right that grants the defendant a fair trial in which, if found guilty, the defendant will be given a sentence or punishment by the judge. This sentence would be considered to be fair based on the offense committed by the offender and the established law of the land which stands as the standard of judgment.

The standard for the judgment of sin in *Eternal Judgment* is the *Word of God*. The *Word of God* stands as the moral compass given to men by God for doctrine, reproof, correction, and instruction in righteousness (2 Timothy 3:16). This same *Word* will be held as the standard in the *Day of Judgment*. The following passages reveal the standard of Judgment.

John 12:48
He who rejects Me, and does not receive My words, has that which judges him—the word that I have spoken will judge him in the last day.

Revelation 20:12
And I saw the dead, small and great, standing before God, and books were opened. And another book was opened, which is the Book of Life. And the dead were judged according to their works, by the things which were written in the books.

James 2:12
So speak and so do as those who will be judged by the law of liberty.

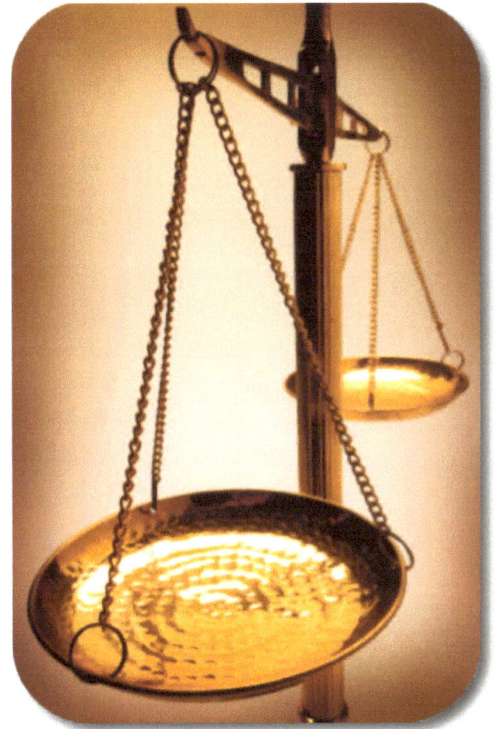

All sin must be judged, and none of creation stands exempt from the judgment of God, not even angels. The Bible teaches that the angels that sinned against God will have their day of judgment also. However, mankind will participate in the judging of angels. The first question that might come to mind is, how will man participate in the judging of angels? Not much detail is given on this besides the fact that we shall judge angels. Apostle Paul in his letter to the Church of Corinth reminds the believers of this fact (1 Corinthians 6:3) as he challenges them to uphold the integrity of the faith in matters of civil judgment among the brethren.

I Corinthians 6:3
Do you not know that we shall judge angels? How much more, things that pertain to this life?

The Bible clearly declares the sins of the angels (Jude 1:6) and the judgment that is and is to come for their disobedience (2 Peter 2:4, 11). The sin of the angels was great, being that it was rebellion against God. The fact that they too shall stand in judgment shows the seriousness of the consequences of sin.

Jude 1:6
And the angels who did not keep their proper domain, but left their own abode

2 Peter 2:4
For if God did not spare the angels who sinned, but cast them down to hell and delivered them into chains of darkness, to be reserved for judgment;

2 Peter 2:11
Whereas angels, which are greater in power and might, bring not railing accusation against them before the Lord.

The Reality Of Sin

The reality of sin is that it must be judged and those who have rebelled against God whether man or angel will have to give an account for their actions. The Bible declares that "*the wages of sin is death*" (Romans 6:23). The same verse goes on to say that the "*gift of God is eternal life*". The *gift* of *Eternal Life* is granted to those who have chosen to live a life pleasing to God.

To bring it all into perspective, the first five books of the Bible authored by Moses are known as the "*Torah*", but it is also referred to as "*The Law*" because of the collection of decrees found within them.[xviii] This collection of writings is referred to all throughout the scriptures as "*The Law*" and by this law the Bible tells us that we have been given *the knowledge of sin* (Romans 3:20). In fact, the Bible defines sin as "*the transgression of the law*" (1 John 3:4).

Romans 3:19-20
Now we know that whatever the law says, it says to those who are under the law, that every mouth may be stopped, and all the world may become guilty before God. 20 Therefore by the deeds of the law no flesh will be justified in His sight, for by the law is the knowledge of sin.

1 John 3:4 (King James Version)
Whosoever committeth sin transgresseth also the law: for sin is the transgression of the law.

1. What does the word judgment mean?

    _____

    _____

2. How can the concepts from a courtroom help us to better understand the
    term, *Eternal Judgment*?

    _____

    _____

3. Who will judge mankind?

    _____

    _____

4. What will mankind be judged for?

    _____

    _____

5. What is the seat that Jesus sits on known as?

    _____

    _____

6. What is the standard used for judgment?

    _____

    _____

7. Who will judge the angels?

    _____

    _____

8. What does the Bible say the angels did?

    _____

    _____

9. What are the first five books of the Bible commonly referred to as?

    _____

    _____

10. How does the Bible define sin?

    _____

    _____

Create an outline that highlights the content covered in this unit. Be sure to include scriptures & detail. Your outline should be able to serve as a roadmap for others.

_____
_____
_____
_____
_____
_____
_____
_____
_____
_____
_____
_____
_____
_____
_____
_____
_____
_____
_____
_____
_____
_____
_____
_____
_____
_____
_____
_____
_____
_____
_____
_____
_____
_____

CONCLUSION

You have completed the "Foundations" Course. At this point you should be knowledgable and able to share many of The Elementary Teachings of Christianity. However, this study by all means does not end here. It should be your hearts desire to obtain a deeper understanding of everything that you have learned so far. Go back and review your answers and outlines and allow the Holy Spirit to lead you in further study of the scriptures. Remember, this is just The Elementary Teachings of Christianity, which are the ingredients for a solid Foundation.

Scan QR Code to access e-Course

FOUNDATION
THE ELEMENTARY TEACHINGS OF CHRISTIANITY

REFERENCES

i Foundation. (2010) MSN Dictionary. from http://encarta.msn.com/

ii Richards, L.O., Richards Complete Bible Dictionary (Iowa Falls: World Bible Publishers, Ink, 2002), 307

iii Richards, L.O., New International Encyclopedia Of Bible Words (Grand Rapids: Zondervan Publishing House, 1991), 522

iv Faith, (2010) MSN Dictionary. from http://encarta.msn.com/

v Substance, (2010) MSN Dictionary. from http://encarta.msn.com/

vi Substance, (2010) Crosswalk. from http://biblestudytools.com/

vii Richards, L.O., Richards Complete Bible Dictionary (Iowa Falls: World Bible Publishers, Ink, 2002), 126

viii Power, (2010) Crosswalk. from http://biblestudytools.com/

ix Resurrection, (2010) Bible Study Tools. from http://biblestudytools.com/

x Resuscitate, (2010) MSN Dictionary. from http://encarta.msn.com/

xi Hades, (2010) Bible Study Tools. from http://biblestudytools.com/

xii Sheol, (2010) Bible Study Tools. from http://biblestudytools.com/

xiii Rapture, (2010) Theopedia. from http://www.theopedia.com /

xiv Rapture, (2010) Bible Study Tools. from http://biblestudytools.com/

xv Judgment, (2010) Bible Study Tools. from http://biblestudytools.com/

xvi Judgment Seat, (2010) Bible Study Tools. from http://biblestudytools.com/

xvii Judgment Seat, (2010) Bible Study Tools. from http://biblestudytools.com/

xviii The Law, (2010) Biblica. from http://www.biblica.com/

ABOUT THE AUTHOR

"Make Disciples"... This simple statement that Jesus commanded His followers has been the driving force behind the ministry of Pastor J. L. Shelton. The structure of his work has been built around being a servant-leader, leading from a position of servitude and equipping men & women of God to participate in the redemption of mankind. His passion has been to reach the unreached and those who are not usually targeted by the traditional methods of outreach.

Pastor J. is a devout student of the Word who finds a fervent love in the teaching of the Scriptures. Although he does not boast or find affirmation in his education, Pastor J. has obtained multiple degrees in his journey over the years. He currently holds an Assoc. Degree in Multi-Media from the Art Institute of Houston, a Dual B.S. Degree in Theology & Christian Ministry from The College of Biblical Studies, a Masters Degree in Education-Curriculum & Instruction and he has also been a student of Religious Studies and Psychology at the University of Houston.

Over the years God has molded Pastor J. in such a way that modern day Churchology would label radical and extreme. Having a heart of a missionary, he has taken the message of the Gospel and aimed it at a culture that has grown dull and desynthesized to the voice of the Church. Pastor J. has stepped out of the box of tradition and sought to walk in the likeness of the Church found in the Book of Acts. He has chosen to take the Word of God literally in all areas and seeks to "Make Disciples" that "Make Disciples".

It has been through his wrestling with God experiences that have birthed a hunger and thirst for the presence of God in his life and ministry. The vision that God has given Pastor J. is one of Revival. A vision of the full restoration of the Glory of God once again resting upon the Church. A vision of the Church fulfilling its evangelistic call of preaching the Gospel to every creature. A vision of the Church united in the unity and love of Jesus Christ & absent of all denominational boundaries.

To Schedule Pastor J for a speaking engagement you can contact him personally at:
J@PastorJ.com
www.PastorJ.com

OTHER RESOURCES BY J.L. SHELTON

Books
Urban Mission Field: A Plea for Revival of Missions
The Garden: A Beautiful Engaging Study of the Garden of GOD
Foundation: The Stone Which the Builders Rejected
The Repent Diet: A Radical Approach to Health & Nutrition
Logos: A comprehensive study of the literal "WORD" of GOD

DVD's
Urban Mission Field
The Black Tape Letters
Testimony
The Mis-Education of the CHURCH

CD's
Change Gonna Come
Spiritual Exodus Vol. 1-3
Revival

www.PastorJ.com
www.Day50Publishing.com

www.ingramcontent.com/pod-product-compliance
Lightning Source LLC
LaVergne TN
LVHW072106070426
835509LV00002B/33